A
Newman Con
for
Sundays and Feastdays

Ring in the love of truth and right,
Ring in the common love of good.
Ring in the valiant man and free
The larger heart, the kindlier hand;
Ring out the darkness of the land;
Ring in the Christ that is to be.

Tennyson *In Memoriam*

Dedicated to the members of Newman's Oratory past and present

A
Newman Compendium
for
Sundays and Feastdays

Edited by

James Tolhurst
of the Oratory

Gracewing.

First published in 1995
Gracewing
Fowler Wright Books
Southern Avenue, Leominster
Herefordshire HR6 0QF

Gracewing Books are distributed

In New Zealand by:
Catholic Supplies Ltd
80 Adelaide Rd
Wellington
New Zealand

In Australia by:
Charles Paine Pty
8 Ferris Street
North Parramatta
NSW 2151 Australia

In U.S.A. by:
Morehouse Publishing
P.O. Box 1321
Harrisburg
PA 17105
U.S.A.

In Canada by:
Meakin and Associates
Unit 17, 81 Auriga Drive
Nepean, Ontario, KZE 7Y5
Canada

cum permissu

Compilation and editorial material © James Tolhurst, *Cong. Orat*

ISBN 0 85244 2920

Cover illustration based on the Westmacott bust in the possession of the Oratory Fathers, Edgbaston
Typesetting by Action Typesetting Limited, Gloucester
Printed by The Cromwell Press, Melksham, Wiltshire

CONTENTS

Preface

Fr. James Tolhurst is to be commended on having produced *A Newman Compendium for Sundays and Feastdays*. This gives us passages from John Henry Newman sermons, mostly from his Anglican pulpit, matched to the readings now appointed for these days. They follow the three year cycle of readings drawn up by the reform of the Roman Missal following the Second Vatican Council. As such, this book provides meditations on Scripture which are full of Newman's insights. It is instructive to see him, bringing together quotations from his wide knowledge of the Bible, and meditating on them in the deliberate Victorian prose which is his own. The Newman Compendium will be appreciated by those who look to the great Cardinal as a spiritual guide and as a sensitive interpreter of the truths and Revelations.

Maurice Couve de Murville
Archbishop of Birmingham

Introduction

A stranger, meeting John Henry Newman in 1861 in Cambridge, said to him "I think I have heard you in the pulpit of St Mary's Oxford some thirty years ago".[1] Such was the impact made by the preacher on his hearers. Not that Newman was in any way dramatic in his mode of delivery: the sermons were read and his eyes were always bent on the manuscript, but people noticed "the solemn sternness", "the music in the tone".[2]

Newman did not pamper his hearers. He intended that they should respond to the demands of the Gospel and wrote that he would send John the Baptist before the face of Christ in the words he uttered.[3] But there would be no ranting, no "yoke of bondage" imposed on them.[4] So it was that "as he spoke the old truth became new... He laid his finger how gently, yet how powerfully, on some inner place in the hearer's heart, and told him things about himself he had never known till then."[5] The effect of such sustained sincerity, was, we are told irresistible and carried people beyond themselves in response to his words.

We must bear this in mind when we read his words. They are communications from the heart of the preacher to the heart of his audience. Sunday by Sunday they came to hear him, undergraduates and townsfolk; and the present selection is arranged for each Sunday of the three year cycle and the principal feasts and holydays of obligation so that his influence can remain with us. Most of the texts are from the *Parochial and Plain Sermons*, "those indestructible classics of English theology" as Gladstone termed them,[6] but the selection ranges from 1828 to 1880.

It was said that when Newman left Oxford, it was as if the great bell of a cathedral had suddenly ceased tolling. But as we can see from these pages his voice was not silenced when 150 years ago on a rainy evening on 8 October, 1845 he welcomed Fr Dominic Barberi to Littlemore and was received into the Catholic Church the following day. Ahead lay the *Discourses to Mixed Congregations*, the Sermons preached before the Catholic University of Ireland and the sermons he preached by invitation (*Christ upon the Waters*, *The Second Spring*...) and week by week to the congregation here in Birmingham. There was the same conviction in his words because he had not changed, and he still spoke from the heart because "nothing anonymous will preach; nothing that is dead and gone; nothing even which is of yesterday; however religious in itself and useful. Thought and word are one in the Eternal Logos, and must issue fresh and fresh, as from the preacher's mouth, so from his breast if they are to be 'spirit and life' to the hearts of his hearers".[7] This can be appreciated if the words are read in the context of the current liturgical readings.

Besides certain additional references I have also added the occasional note for an audience that might not be as familiar with the Bible as was his congregation. But I have made no change to the words of the *Authorized Version*, for Newman weaves his text round those sonorous phrases. My thanks go to Gerard Tracey, Birmingham Oratory Archivist.

May Newman's voice inspire in us his deep commitment whether we preach or whether we hear the word of God: "It is by You that sinners are turned into saints. It is by You the Church is refreshed and strengthened".[8]

Edgbaston, Feast of Saint Philip Neri, 1995
James Tolhurst

1   Quoted in *Newman, Light in Winter*, Meriol Trevor, London, 1962, p. 248.
2   Gladstone speaking in the City Temple, 1877 (quoted *Daily Chronicle*, 12 August, 1980)
3   Newman writing to James Stephen, 16 March, 1835, LD, V, p. 47.
4   *Jfc*, p. 365.
5   *John Keble*, J C Shairp, Edinburgh, 1866, p. 17.
6   *Vaticanism*, 1874, p. 12.
7   *Idea*, p. 426.
8   MD, p. 547.

Part I:
Sundays of the Year

First Sunday of Advent

Isa 2, 1−5; Rom 13, 11−14; Matt 24, 37−44

'So, stay awake ...'

Hence it follows, that watching is a special mark of the Scripture Christian, as our Lord so emphatically sets before us: 'Watch therefore, for ye know not what hour your Lord doth come. ... Be ye also ready, for in such an hour as ye think not the Son of man cometh.'[1] 'At midnight there was a cry made, Behold, the bridegroom cometh, go ye out to meet Him. ... Watch therefore, for ye know neither the day nor the hour wherein the Son of man cometh.'[2] 'Watch ye therefore, for ye know not when the Master of the house cometh, at even, or at midnight, or at the cockcrowing, or in the morning; lest coming suddenly he find you sleeping; and what I say unto you, I say unto all, Watch.'[3] And St. Peter, who once suffered for lack of watching, repeats the lesson: 'The end of all things is at hand: be ye therefore sober, and watch unto prayer.'[4]

The Apostolical Christian   SD p. 279−80.   February 5 or 12, 1843

1   Matt. 24, 42−44
2   Matt. 25, 6−13
3   Mark 13, 35−37
4   1 Pet. 4, 7

Second Sunday of Advent

Isa 11, 1–10; Rom 15, 4–9; Matt 3, 1–12

'... In the Spirit and Power of Elijah'

Elijah was the foremost, and in one sense the beginning of the Prophets; and, whereas he is so prominent in the Old Testament, he is not less prominent in the New; for he has come to the Church, as if over again, in the person of St. John the Baptist, of whom it was prophesied before his birth, that he should go before our Lord, 'in the spirit and power of Elias,' to 'turn the heart of the fathers to the children, and the heart of the children to their fathers'; and whom we twice commemorate in the course of the year; — at one time praying that 'after his example we may constantly speak the truth, boldly rebuke vice, and patiently suffer for the truth's sake'; at the other, that, as he was sent as a messenger, to prepare Christ's way, so the ministers and stewards of His mysteries may so turn 'the hearts of the disobedient to the wisdom of the just, that at His second coming we may be found an acceptable people in His sight.'

Elijah the Prophet of the Latter Days   SD p. 367–8.   February 26, 1843

Third Sunday of Advent

Isa 35, 1–6.10; Jas 5, 7–10; Matt 11, 2–11

'Then what did you go out to see?'

The Holy Baptist was separated from the world. He was a Nazarite. He went out from the world, and placed himself over against it, and spoke to it from his vantage ground, and called it to repentance. Then went out all Jerusalem to him into the desert, and he confronted it face to face. But in his teaching he spoke of One who should come to them and speak to them in a far different way. He should not separate Himself from them. He should not display Himself as some higher being, but as their brother, as of their flesh and of their bones, as one among many brethren, as one of the multitude and amidst them; nay, He was among them already. *'Medius vestrum stetit, quem vos nescitis'*[1] – 'there hath stood in the midst of you, whom you know not.' That greater one called Himself the Son of man – He was content to be taken as ordinary in all respects, though He was the Highest. St. John and the other Evangelists, though so different in the character of their accounts of Him, agree most strikingly here. The Baptist says, 'There is in the midst of you One whom you know not.'

God with us   MD p. 489–90

---

1   John 1, 26

Fourth Sunday of Advent

Isa 7, 10–14; Rom 1, 1–7; Matt 1, 18–24

'The Virgin will conceive and give birth to a Son'

I have been speaking of the signs which He Himself promised; but others were announced concerning Him by His servants, and these, let it be observed, are secret also, and addressed to faith. The Prophet Isaiah was commissioned to promise Ahaz a sign; 'Ask thee a sign of the Lord thy God,' he says, 'ask it either in the depth or in the height above.' When Ahaz would not speak, the Prophet proceeded: 'The Lord Himself shall give you a Sign; behold, a Virgin shall conceive, and bear a Son, and shall call His name Immanuel.'[1] Yet could there be a Sign more secret, less exposed to the senses, less addressed to the reason, than the Conception of Christ? It was a miracle, yet not an evidence.

And so again, when our Lord was born, the Angel gave the Shepherds a Sign; but which was the greater evidence, the Angel himself, and the multitude of the heavenly host, or the Sign itself which he sent them to see? 'This shall be a Sign unto you,' he said, 'Ye shall see the Babe wrapped in swaddling clothes, lying in a manger.' Was this an evidence of greatness or of meanness? Did it prove Him to be God, or was it a trial of faith?

The Gospel Sign addressed to Faith   PPS VI p. 111–112.   12/26 November 1837

---

1   Isa 7, 11. 14

Christmas Midnight Mass

Isa 9, 1–7; Titus 2, 11–14; Luke 2, 1–14

She gave birth to a Son and laid him in a Manger

'The shepherds said one to another, Let us now go even unto Bethlehem, and see this thing which is come to pass, which the Lord hath made known to us.' Let us too go with them, to contemplate that second and greater miracle to which the Angel directed them, the Nativity of Christ. St. Luke says of the Blessed Virgin, 'She brought forth her first-born Son, and wrapped Him in swaddling clothes, and laid Him in a manger.' What a wonderful sign is this to all the world, and therefore the Angel repeated it to the shepherds: 'Ye shall find the babe wrapped in swaddling clothes, lying in a manger.' The God in heaven and earth, the Divine Word, who had been in glory with the Eternal Father from the beginning, He was at this time born into this world of sin as a little infant. He, as at this time, lay in His mother's arms, to all appearance helpless and powerless, and was wrapped by Mary in an infant's bands, and laid to sleep in a manger. The Son of God Most High, who created the worlds, became flesh, though remaining what He was before. He became flesh as truly as if He had ceased to be what He was, and had actually been changed into flesh. He submitted to be the offspring of Mary, to be taken up in the hands of a mortal, to have a mother's eye fixed upon Him, and to be cherished at a mother's bosom. A daughter of man became the Mother of God — to her, indeed, an unspeakable gift of grace; but in Him what condescension! What an emptying of His glory to become man! and not only a helpless infant, though that were humiliation enough, but to inherit all the infirmities and imperfections of our nature which were possible to a sinless soul. What were His thoughts, if we may venture to use such language or admit such a reflection concerning the Infinite, when human feelings, human sorrows, human wants, first became His? What a mystery is there from first to last in the Son of God becoming man! Yet in proportion to the mystery is the grace and mercy of it; and as is the grace, so is the greatness of the fruit of it.

Religious Joy   PPS VIII p. 251–2.   March 13, 1836

Christmas Dawn Mass

Isa 62, 11–12; Titus 3, 4–7; Luke 2, 15–20

They found Mary and Joseph and the Baby lying in the Manger

If any there was who might seem to have permission to indulge in words on this subject, it was the beloved disciple, who had heard and seen, and looked upon, and handled the Word of Life; yet, in proportion to the height of his privilege, was his discernment of the infinite distance between him and his Creator. Such too was the temper of the Holy Angels, when the Father 'brought in the First-begotten into the world:'[1] they straightway worshipped Him. And such was the feeling of awe and love mingled together, which remained for a while in the Church after Angels had announced His coming, and Evangelists had recorded His sojourn here, and His departure; 'there was silence as it were for half an hour.'[2] Around the Church, indeed, the voices of blasphemy were heard, even as when He hung on the cross; but in the Church there was light and peace, fear, joy, and holy meditation. Lawless doubtings, importunate inquirings, confident reasonings were not. An heartfelt adoration, a practical devotion to the Ever-blessed Son, precluded difficulties in faith, and sheltered the Church from the necessity of speaking.

Christmas Day   The Incarnation   PPS II p. 26–7.   25 December, 1834

1   Heb. 1, 6
2   Rev. 8, 1

What were the actual circumstances of His coming? His mother is a poor woman; she comes to Bethlehem to be taxed, travelling, when her choice would have been to remain at home. She finds there is no room in the inn; she is obliged to betake herself to a stable; she brings forth her firstborn Son, and lays Him in a manger. That little babe, so born, so placed, is none other than the Creator of heaven and earth, the Eternal Son of God.

Christ Hidden from the World   PPS IV p. 240–1.   25 December, 1837

Let us then, according to the light given us, praise and bless Him in the Church below, whom Angels in heaven see and adore. Let us bless Him for His surpassing loving-kindness in taking upon Him our infirmities to redeem us, when he dwelt in the inner-most love of the Everlasting Father, in the glory which He had with Him before the world was. He came in lowliness and want; born amid the tumults of a mixed and busy multitude, cast aside into the outhouse of a crowded inn, laid to His first rest among the brute cattle.

Christmas Day   The Incarnation   PPS II p. 38–9.   25 December, 1834

Christmas Day Mass

Isa 52, 7–10; Heb 1, 1–6; John 1, 1–18

'The Word was made flesh'

The great safeguard to the doctrine of our Lord's Divinity is the doctrine of His Sonship; we realize that He is God only when we acknowledge Him to be by nature and from eternity Son.

Nay, our Lord's Sonship is not only the guarantee to us of His Godhead, but also the condition of His incarnation. As the Son was God, so on the other hand was the Son suitably made man; it belonged to Him to have the Father's perfections, it became Him to assume a servant's form ...

... He was a Son both before His incarnation, and, by a second mystery, after it. From eternity He had been the Only-begotten in the bosom of the Father; and when He came on earth, this essential relation to the Father remained unaltered; still, He was a Son, when in the form of a servant, – still performing the will of the Father, as His Father's Word and Wisdom, manifesting His Father's glory and accomplishing His Father's purposes.

Christ, the Son of God made Man   PPS VI p. 58–9.   26 April, 1836

The Word was from the beginning, the Only-begotten Son of God. Before all worlds were created, while as yet time was not, He was in existence, in the bosom of the Eternal Father, God from God, and Light from Light, supremely blessed in knowing and being known of Him, and receiving all divine perfections from him, yet ever One with Him who begat Him. As it is said in the opening of the Gospel: 'In the beginning was the Word, and the Word was with God, and the Word was God.' If we may dare conjecture, He is called the Word of God, as mediating between the Father and all creatures; bringing them into being, fashioning them, giving the world its laws, imparting reason and conscience to creatures of a higher order, and revealing to them in due season and knowledge of God's will. And to us Christians He is especially the Word in that great mystery commemorated to-day, whereby he became flesh, and redeemed us from a state of sin.

He, indeed, when man fell, might have remained in the glory which He had with the Father before the world was. But that unsearchable Love, which showed itself in our original creation, rested not content with a frustrated work, but brought Him down again from His Father's bosom to do His will, and repair the evil which sin had caused. And with a wonderful condescension He came, not as before in power, but in weakness, in the form of a servant, in the likeness of that fallen creature whom He purposed to restore. So He humbled Himself; suffering all the infirmities of our nature in the likeness of sinful flesh, all but a sinner, − pure from all sin, yet subjected to all temptation, − and at length becoming obedient unto death, even the death of the cross.

Christmas Day   The Incarnation   PPS II p. 29. 30.   25 December, 1834

Sunday in the Octave of Christmas: The Holy Family

Sir 3, 2–6. 12–14; Col 3, 12–21; Matt 2, 13–15. 19–23

'*. . . Because Herod intends to search for the Child to destroy him*'

And, independently of the benefit thus accruing to us, it is surely right and meet thus to celebrate the death of the Holy Innocents: for it was a blessed one. To be brought near to Christ, and to suffer for Christ, is surely an unspeakable privilege; to suffer anyhow, even unconsciously. The little children whom He took up in his arms, were not conscious of His loving condescension; but was it no privilege when He blessed them? Surely this massacre had in it the nature of a Sacrament; it was a pledge of the love of the Son of God towards those who were included in it. All who came near Him, more or less suffered by approaching Him, just as if earthly pain and trouble went out of Him, as some precious virtue for the good of their souls; – and these infants in the number. Surely His very presence was a Sacrament; every motion, look, and word of His conveying grace to those who would receive it: and much more was fellowship with Him. And hence in ancient times such barbarous murders or Martyrdoms were considered as a kind of baptism, a baptism of blood, with a sacramental charm in it, which stood in the place of the appointed Laver of regeneration. Let us then take these little children as in some sense Martyrs, and see what instruction we may gain from the pattern of their innocence.

Holy Innocents. The Mind of Little Children   PPS II p. 62.   28 December, 1833

1 January: Solemnity of Mary, Mother of God

Num 6, 22–27; Gal 4, 4–7; Luke 2, 16–21

Mary pondered these things in her heart

Mary's faith did not end in a mere acquiescence in Divine providences and revelations: as the text informs us, she 'pondered' them. When the shepherds came, and told of the vision of Angels which they had seen at the time of the Nativity, and how one of them announced that the Infant in her arms was 'the Saviour, which is Christ the Lord,' while others did but wonder, 'Mary kept all these things, and pondered them in her heart.' Again, when her Son and Saviour had come to the age of twelve years, and had left her for awhile for His Father's service, and had been found, to her surprise, in the Temple, amid the doctors, both hearing them and asking them questions, and had, on her addressing Him, vouchsafed to justify His conduct, we are told, 'His mother kept all these sayings in her heart.' And accordingly, at the marriage-feast in Cana, her faith anticipated His first miracle, and she said to the servants, 'Whatsoever He saith unto you, do it.'

Thus St. Mary is our pattern of Faith, both in the reception and in the study of Divine Truth. She does not think it enough to accept, she dwells upon it; not enough to possess, she uses it; not enough to assent, she develops it; not enough to submit the Reason, she reasons upon it; not indeed reasoning first, and believing afterwards, with Zacharias, yet first believing without reasoning, next from love and reverence, reasoning after believing. And thus she symbolizes to us, not only the faith of the unlearned, but of the doctors of the Church also, who have to investigate, and weigh, and define, as well as to profess the Gospel.

The Theory of Developments   US p. 312–3.   2 February, 1843

Second Sunday after Christmas

Sir 24, 1–2. 12–16; Eph 1, 3–6. 15–18; John 1, 1–18

'... and the Word was with God in the beginning'

Thus He came into this world, not in the clouds of heaven, but born into it, born of a woman; He, the Son of Mary, and she (if it may be said), the mother of God. Thus He came, selecting and setting apart for Himself the elements of body and soul; then, uniting them to Himself from their first origin of existence, pervading them, hallowing them by His own Divinity, spiritualizing them, and filling them with light and purity, the while they continued to be human, and for a time mortal and exposed to infirmity. And, as they grew from day to day in their holy union, His Eternal Essence still was one with them, exalting them, acting in them, manifesting Itself through them, so that He was truly God and Man, One Person, – as we are soul and body, yet one man, so truly God and man are not two, but One Christ. Thus did the Son of God enter this mortal world; and when He had reached man's estate, He began His ministry, preached the Gospel, chose His Apostles, suffered on the cross, died, and was buried, rose again and ascended on high, there to reign till the day when He comes again to judge the world. This is the All-gracious Mystery of the Incarnation, good to look into, good to adore; according to the saying in the text, 'The Word was made flesh, – and dwelt among us.'

Christmas Day   The Incarnation   PPS II p. 31–2.   25 December, 1834

The Epiphany of the Lord

Isa 60, 1–6; Eph 3, 2–3. 5–6; Matt 2, 1–12

'We saw his Star as it rose and have come to worship him'

The day on which we commemorate this gracious appointment of God's Providence, is called the Epiphany, or bright manifestation of Christ to the Gentiles; being the day on which the wise men came from the East under guidance of a star, to worship Him, and thus became the first-fruits of the heathen world. The name is explained by the words of the text, which occur in one of the lessons selected for to-day's service, and in which the Church is addressed. 'Arise, shine; for thy light is come, and the glory of the Lord is risen upon thee. For, behold, the darkness shall cover the earth, and gross darkness the people: but the Lord shall arise upon thee, and His glory shall be seen upon thee. And the Gentiles shall come to thy light, and kings to the brightness of thy rising. ... Thy people also shall be all righteous: they shall inherit the land for ever, the branch of My planting, the work of My hands, that I may be glorified.'[1]

That this and other similar prophecies had their measure of fulfilment when Christ came, we all know; when His Church, built upon the Apostles and Prophets, wonderfully branched out from Jerusalem as a centre into the heathen world round about, and gathering into it men of all ranks, languages, and characters, moulded them upon one pattern, the pattern of their Saviour, in truth and righteousness. Thus the prophecies concerning the Church were fulfilled at that time in two respects, as regards its sanctity and its Catholicity.

The Epiphany   The Glory of the Christian Church   PPS II p. 80–1.
29 November, 1834

---

1   Isa 60, 1. 3. 21

The Baptism of the Lord (First Sunday after Epiphany)

Isa 42, 1–4. 6–7; Acts 10, 34–38; Matt 3, 13–17

'This is my Beloved Son'

Surely we have forgotten, in good measure, the difference between
Jewish Ordinances and Christian. They were as the forerunners in a
procession, who, after announcing their Prince's coming, must
themselves retire, or they crowd his path. Nor these alone, but all
mere ceremonies were then for ever unseasonable, as mere obstacles
intercepting the Divine light. Yet, while Christ abolished them,
considered as means of expiation or mere badges of profession, or as
prophetical types of what was no longer future, He introduced
another class of ordinances in their stead; Mysteries, as they are
sometimes called, among which are the Sacraments, viz., rites as
valueless and powerless in themselves as the Jewish, but being, what
the Jewish were not, instruments of the application of His merits to
individual believers. Though He now sits on the right hand of God,
He has, in one sense, never left the world since He first entered it; for,
by the ministration of the Holy Ghost, He is really present with us in
an unknown way, and ever imparts Himself to those who seek Him.
Even when visibly on earth He, the Son of Man, was still 'in heaven';
and now, though He is ascended on high, He is still on earth. And as
He is still with us, for all that He is in heaven, so, again, is the hour
of His cross and passion ever mystically present, though it be past
these eighteen hundred years. Time and space have no portion in the
spiritual Kingdom which he has founded; and the rites of His Church
are as mysterious spells by which He annuls them both. They are not
like the Jewish ordinances, all. Once for all he hung upon the cross,
and blood and water issued from His pierced side, but by the Spirit's
ministration, the blood and water are ever flowing, as though His
cross were really set up among us, and the baptismal water were but
an outward image meeting our senses. Thus in a true sense that water
is not what it was before, but is gifted with new and spiritual qualities.
Not as if its material substance were changed, which our eyes see, or
as if any new nature were imparted to it, but that the lifegiving Spirit,
who could make bread of stones, and sustain animal life on dust and

ashes, applies the blood of Christ through it; or according to the doctrine of the text, that He, and not man, is the baptizer.

Regenerating Baptism   PPS III p. 276—7. 8.   15 November, 1835

First Sunday of Lent

Gen 2, 7–9. 3, 1–7; Rom 5, 12–19; Matt 4, 1–11

'He was tempted as we are but did not sin'

And this anticipation is confirmed by the history of our Lord's temptation in the wilderness. It *began*, you will observe, with an attempt on the part of the evil one to make Him break His fast improperly. It *began*, but it did not end there. It was but the first of three temptations, and the other two were more addressed to His mind, not His bodily wants. One was to throw Himself down from the pinnacle, the other the offer of all the kingdoms of the world. They were more subtle temptations. Now, I have used the word 'subtle' already, and it needs some explanation. By a subtle temptation or a subtle sin, I mean one which it is very difficult to find out. Everyone knows what it is to break the ten commandments, the first, the second, the third, and so on. When a thing is directly commanded and the devil tempts us directly to break it, this is *not* a subtle temptation but a broad and gross temptation. But there are a great many things wrong which are not so obviously wrong. They are wrong as leading to what is wrong or the consequence of what is wrong, or they are wrong because they are the very same thing as what is forbidden, but dressed up and looking differently. The human mind is very deceitful; when a thing is forbidden, a man does not like directly to do it, but he goes to work if he can to get at the forbidden end in some way.

Surrender to God   CS p. 70–1.   5 March, 1878. St Chad's, Birmingham

And as the doctrine of our Lord's humiliation is most mysterious, so the very surface of the narrative in which it is contained is mysterious also, as exciting wonder, and impressing upon us our real ignorance of the nature, manner, and causes of it. Take, for instance, His temptation. Why was it undergone at all, seeing our redemption is ascribed to His death, not to it? Why was it so long? What took place during it? What was Satan's particular object in tempting Him? How came Satan to have such power over Him as to be able to transport Him from place to place? and what was the precise result of the temptation? These and many other questions admit of no satisfactory solution. There is something remarkable too in the period of it, being the same as that of the long fasts of Moses and Elijah, and of His own abode on earth after His resurrection. A like mystery again is cast around that last period of His earthly mission. Then he was engaged we know not how, except that He appeared, from time to time, to His Apostles; of the forty days of His temptation we know still less, only that 'He did eat nothing,' and 'was with the wild beasts'.[1]

The Humiliation of the Eternal Son   PPS III p. 157–8.   8 March, 1835

---

1   Luke 4. 2; Mark 1. 13

Second Sunday of Lent

Gen 12, 1–4; 2 Tim 1. 8–10; Matt 17, 1–9

'Lord, it is good for us to be here'

Our Lord often passed the night in prayer, and as afterwards in that sad night before His Passion He took with Him three Apostles to witness His prayer in agony, so at an earlier time He took the same favoured three with Him to witness His prayer in ecstasy and glory. On the one occasion He fell on His face and prayed more earnestly till He was covered with a sweat of blood which rolled down upon the cold earth. In the other, as He prayed His countenance became bright and glorious, and He was lifted off the earth. So He remained communing with His Father, ministered to by Moses and Elias, till a voice came from the cloud, which said: 'This is My beloved Son, hear ye Him.' The sight had been so wonderful, so transporting, that St. Peter could not help crying out. He knew not what he said. He did not know how to express his inward feelings, nor did he understand in a moment all the wonders about him. He could but say: 'Lord, it is good for us to be here'. Simple words, but how much they contain in them. It was good, it was the good of man, it was the great good, it was our good. He did not say that the sight was sublime and marvellous. He was not able to reflect upon it and describe it. His reason did not speak, but his affections. He did but say that it was good to be there. And he wished that great good to continue to him ever. He said: 'Let us build three tabernacles, one for Thee, one for Moses, and one for Elias'. He wished to remain there for ever, it was so good. He was loath the vision should come to an end. He did not like to descend from the mount and return to those whom he had left behind.

The World and Sin   CS p. 80–1.   2nd Sunday in Lent, 1848. St. Chad's, Birmingham

Therefore is it good to throw ourselves into the unseen world, it is 'good to be there', and to build tabernacles for those who speak 'a pure language' and 'serve the Lord with one consent'

The Intermediate State   Cf. Feast of the Transfiguration PPS III p. 386.
1 November, 1835

Third Sunday of Lent

Exod 17, 3–7; Rom 5, 1–2. 5–8; John 4, 5–42

'If you knew the Gift of God ...'

There was one occasion when our Saviour said, 'The hour cometh, when ye shall neither in this mountain, nor yet at Jerusalem, worship the Father. The hour cometh, when the true worshippers shall worship the Father in spirit and in truth'. Did we take these words by themselves, we might consider they implied, that, under the Gospel, there would be no outward tokens of religion, no rites and ordinances at all, no public services, no assemblings of ourselves together, and, especially, no sacred buildings. Such an inference, however, would be a great error, if it were only for this reason, that it has never been received, never acted on in any age of the Church; so far from it, that I suppose there are few indeed but would shrink from the very mention of it, and none at all who could be found to testify that they had adopted it in their own case, yet had not suffered from it in point of inward devotion to God's service. That cannot be the true sense of Scripture, which never has been fulfilled, which ever has been contradicted and disobeyed; for God's word shall not return unto Him void, but shall accomplish His pleasure and prosper in His purpose. Our Saviour did *not* say to the Samaritan woman that there should be no places and buildings for worship under the Gospel, *because* He has *not* brought it to pass, *because* such ever have been, at all times and in all countries, and amid all differences of faith. And the same reasons which lead us to believe that religious edifices are a Christian ordinance, though so very little is said about them in Scripture, will also show that it is right and pious to make them enduring, and stately, and magnificent, and ornamental; so that our Saviour's declaration, when he foretold the destruction of the Temple at Jerusalem, was not that there should never be any other house built to His honour, but rather that there should be many houses; that they should be built, not merely at Jerusalem, or at Gerizim, but every where; what was under the Law a local ordinance, being henceforth a Catholic privilege, allowed not here and there, but wherever was the Spirit and the Truth. The glory of the Gospel is not the *abolition* of rites, but their *dissemination*; not their absence, but their living and efficacious presence through the grace of Christ.

The Gospel Palaces PPS VI p. 270−1. 13 November, 1836

Now what has been said, little as it is to what might be brought together on the subject, may suffice to suggest to us that great privilege which we may enjoy if we seek it, of dwelling in a heavenly home in the midst of this turbulent world. The world is no helpmeet for man, and a helpmeet he needs.

... What is our resource? It is not in arm of man, in flesh and blood, in voice of friend, or in pleasant countenance; it is that holy home which God has given us in His Church; it is that everlasting City in which he has fixed His abode. It is that Mount invisible whence Angels are looking at us with their piercing eyes, and the voices of the dead call us. 'Greater is He that is in us than he that is in the world'; 'If God be for us, who can be against us?'[1]

Great privilege indeed, if we did but realize its greatness! Man seeks the Creator; let us 'seek the Lord and His strength, seek His face evermore'[2] Let us turn from the world, let us hide ourselves in His dwelling-place.

The Church a Home for the Lonely PPS IV p. 195−6. 22 October, 1837

---

1 1 John 4, 4; Rom 8, 31
2 Ps 105, 4 (B.C.P.)

Fourth Sunday of Lent

1 Sam 16, 1. 6−7. 10−13; Eph 5, 8−14; John 9, 1−41

A Spring of Living Water

This wonderful change from darkness to light, through the entrance of the Spirit into the soul, is called Regeneration, or the New Birth; a blessing which, before Christ's coming, not even Prophets and righteous men possessed, but which is now conveyed to all men freely through the Sacrament of Baptism. By nature we are children of wrath; the heart is sold under sin, possessed by evil spirits; and inherits death as its eternal portion. But by the coming of the Holy Ghost, all guilt and pollution are burned away as by fire, the devil is driven forth, sin, original and actual, is forgiven, and the whole man is consecrated to God. And this is the reason why He is called 'the earnest' of that Saviour who died for us, and will one day give us the fullness of His own presence in heaven. Hence, too, He is our 'seal unto the day of redemption';[1] for as the potter moulds the clay, so He impresses the Divine image on us members of the household of God. And His work may truly be called Regeneration; for though the original nature of the soul is not destroyed, yet its past transgressions are pardoned once and for ever, and its source of evil staunched and gradually dried up by the pervading health and purity which has set up its abode in it. Instead of its own bitter waters, a spring of health and salvation is brought within it; not the mere streams of the fountain, 'clear as crystal', which is before the Throne of God,[2] but, as our Lord says, 'a well of water *in him*', in a man's heart, 'springing up into everlasting life'. Hence He elsewhere describes the heart as giving forth, not receiving, the streams of grace: 'Out of his belly shall flow rivers of Living Water.'

Whitsunday   The Indwelling Spirit   PPS II p. 223−4.   Nov/Dec 1834

1   Eph 1, 14. 4, 30
2   Rev 4, 6; Ps 46, 4

When 'He spat on the ground, and made clay of the spittle, and He anointed the eyes of the blind man with the clay,' He exerted the virtue of His Divine Essence through the properties and circumstances of the flesh. When he breathed on His disciples and said, 'Receive ye the Holy Ghost',[1] He vouchsafed to give His Holy Spirit through the breath of His human nature. When virtue went out of Him, so that whoso touched Him was made whole, here too, in like manner, He shows us that He was not an individual man, like any of us, but God acting through human nature as His assumed instrument.

Christ, the Son of God made Man   PPS VI p. 63.   26 April, 1836

1   John 20, 22

Fifth Sunday of Lent

Ezek 37, 12–14; Rom 8, 8–11; John 11, 1–45

'Lazarus, come forth ...'

Alas! there were other thoughts still to call forth His tears. This marvellous benefit to the forlorn sisters, how was it to be attained? at His own cost. Joseph knew he could bring joy to his brethren, but at no sacrifice of his own. Christ was bringing life to the dead by His own death. His disciples would have dissuaded Him from going into Judea, *lest* the Jews should kill Him. Their apprehension was fulfilled. He went to raise Lazarus, and the fame of that miracle was the immediate cause of His seizure and crucifixion. This He knew beforehand, He saw the prospect before Him; He saw Lazarus raised; the supper in Martha's house; Lazarus sitting at table; joy on all sides of Him; Mary honouring her Lord on this festive occasion by the out-pouring of the very costly ointment upon His feet; the Jews crowding not only to see Him, but Lazarus also; His triumphant entry into Jerusalem; the multitude shouting Hosanna; the people testifying to the raising of Lazarus; the Greeks, who had come up to worship at the feast, earnest to see Him; the children joining in the general joy; and then the Pharisees plotting against Him, Judas betraying Him, His friends deserting Him and the cross receiving Him. These things doubtless, among a multitude of thoughts unspeakable, passed over His mind. He felt that Lazarus was wakening to life at His own sacrifice; that He was descending into the grave which Lazarus left. He felt that Lazarus was to live and He to die; the appearance of things was to be reversed; the feast was to be kept in Martha's house, but the last passover of sorrow remained for Him. And He knew that this reverse was altogether voluntary with Him. He had come down from His Father's bosom to be an Atonement of blood for all sin, and thereby to raise all believers from the grave, as He was then about to raise Lazarus; and to raise them, not for a time, but for eternity ...

Tears of Christ at the grave of Lazarus   PPS III p. 136–7.   12 April, 1835

Passion Sunday (Palm Sunday)

Isa 50, 4–7; Phil 2, 6–11; Matt 26, 14–27. 66

'... A Body hast thou fitted to me'

Consequently, when He determined to suffer the pain of His vicarious passion, whatever He did, He did, as the Wise Man says, *instanter*, 'earnestly', with His might; He did not do it by halves; He did not turn away His mind from the suffering as we do − (how should He, who came to suffer, who could not have suffered but of His own act?) no, He did not say and unsay, do and undo; He said and He did; He said, 'Lo, I come to do Thy will, O God; sacrifice and offering Thou wouldest not, but a body hast Thou fitted to Me'.[1] He took a body in order that He might suffer; He became man, that He might suffer as man; and when His hour was come, that hour of Satan and of darkness, the hour when sin was to pour its full malignity upon Him, it followed that He offered Himself wholly, a holocaust, a whole burnt-offering; − as the whole of His body, stretched out upon the Cross, so the whole of His soul, His whole advertence, His whole consciousness, a mind awake, a sense acute, a living co-operation, a present, absolute intention, not a virtual permission, not a heartless submission, this did He present to His tormentors. His passion was an action; He lived most energetically, while He lay languishing, fainting, and dying. Nor did He die, except by an act of the will; for He bowed His head, in command as well as in resignation, and said, 'Father, into Thy hands I commend My Spirit'; He gave the word, He surrendered His soul, He did not lose it.

Mental Sufferings of our Lord in His Passion   *Mix* p. 330–1 (Discourse 16).   1849

---

1   Heb 10, 6–7; Ps 40, 6–7

Holy Thursday: Evening Mass of the Lord's Supper

Exod 12, 1–8. 11–14; 1 Cor 11, 23–26; John 13, 1–15

'I will keep the Passover with my Disciples'

There is something very observable and very touching in the earnestness displayed in these words of our Lord, and in the acts which preceded them. He had showed beforehand that great desire, of which He here speaks. That He had thought much of His last passover which He was to eat with His disciples, is plain from the solemnity with which He marked out the place to them, and the display of supernatural knowledge with which he accompanied His directions. "He sendeth forth two of His disciples, Peter and John, and saith unto them, Go ye into the city, and there shall meet you a man bearing a pitcher of water: follow him. And wheresoever he shall go in, say ye to the good-man of the house, The Master saith, My time is at hand; My time is at hand, I will keep the passover at thy house with My disciples. And he shall show you a large upper room furnished; there make ready." And then, "when the hour was come, He sat down, and the twelve Apostles with Him. And He said unto them, With desire I have desired to eat this passover with you before I suffer. For I say unto you, I will not any more eat thereof, until it be fulfilled in the kingdom of God".

You may say, indeed, that most important occurrences took place at that feast; and that these He had in view when He gave the command to prepare for it, and when He expressed His satisfaction in celebrating it. Then He washed His disciples' feet, and gave the precept of humility; then He laid down the great note of the Church, brotherly love, impressing it on them most persuasively by His own example; and then He instituted His own heavenly Sacrament, which was to remain on earth, together with that humility and love, unto the end. It is true; but still it is true also, that he chose a festive occasion as the season for these solemn and gracious acts. He closed His earthly ministry, He parted with His disciples, He entered upon His trial, at a feast. The Son of Man had come, in His own words, eating and drinking; and He preserved this peculiarity of His mission unto the end.

Our Lord's Last Supper and His First   SD p. 27–8.   26 February, 1843

O generous love! that he who smote
In man for man the foe,
The double agony in man
For man should undergo;
And in the garden secretly,
And on the cross on high,
Should teach His brethren and inspire
To suffer and to die.

Dream of Gerontius VV p. 360. January, 1865

Good Friday: Celebration of the Lord's Passion

Isa 52, 13–53, 12; Heb 4, 14–16. 5, 7–9; John 18, 1–19. 42

'A Man of Sorrows ... ours were the sufferings he bore'

Now I bid you consider that that Face, so ruthlessly smitten, was the Face of God Himself; the Brows bloody with the thorns, the sacred Body exposed to view and lacerated with the scourge, the Hands nailed to the Cross, and, afterwards, the Side pierced with the spear; it was the Blood, and the sacred Flesh, and the Hands, and the Temples, and the Side, and the Feet of God Himself, which the frenzied multitude then gazed upon. This is so fearful to thought, that when the mind first masters it, surely it will be difficult to think of any thing else; so that, while we think of it, we must pray God to temper it to us, and to give us strength to think of it rightly, lest it be too much for us.

Taking into account, then, that Almighty God Himself, God the Son, was the Sufferer, we shall understand better than we have hitherto the description given of Him by the Evangelists; we shall see the meaning of His general demeanour, His silence, and the words He used when he spoke, and Pilate's awe at Him.

Yes, we shall all of us, for weal or for woe, one day see that holy Countenance which wicked men struck and dishonoured; we shall see those Hands that were nailed to the cross; that Side which was pierced. We shall see all this; and it will be the sight of the Living God.

This being the great mystery of Christ's Cross and Passion, we might with reason suppose, as I have said, that some great thing would result from it. The sufferings and death of the Word Incarnate could not pass away like a dream; they could not be a mere martyrdom, or a mere display or figure of something else, they must have a virtue in them. This we might be sure of, though nothing had been told us about the result. But that result is also revealed: it is this – our reconciliation to God, the expiation of our sins, and our new creation in holiness.

The Incarnate Son, a Sufferer and Sacrifice   PPS VI p. 74. 76–7.   1 April, 1836

O my great God, Thou hast humbled Thyself, Thou hast stooped to take our flesh and blood, and hast been lifted up upon the tree! I praise and glorify Thee tenfold the more, because Thou hast shown Thy power by means of Thy suffering, than hadst Thou carried on Thy work without it. It is worthy of Thy infinitude thus to surpass and transcend all our thoughts.

The Power of the Cross   MD p. 474

Easter Vigil: Mass of Easter Night

*Rom 6, 3–11; Matt 28, 1–10

'His Face was like lightning, his Robe white as snow'.

And if such was His visible Majesty, while He yet was subject to temptation, infirmity, and pain, much more abundant was the manifestation of His Godhead, when He was risen from the dead. Then the Divine Essence streamed forth (so to say) on every side, and environed His Manhood, as in a cloud of glory. So transfigured was His Sacred Body, that He who had deigned to be born of a woman, and to hang upon the cross, had subtle virtue in Him, like a spirit, to pass through the closed doors to His assembled followers; while, by condescending to the trial of their senses, He showed that it was no mere spirit, but He Himself, as before, with wounded hands and pierced side, who spoke to them. He manifested Himself to them, in this His exalted state, that they might be His witnesses to the people; witnesses of those separate truths which man's reason cannot combine, that He had a real human body, that it was partaker in the properties of His Soul, and that it was inhabited by the Eternal Word. They handled Him, – they saw Him come and go, when the doors were shut, – they felt, what they could not see, but could witness even unto death, that He was 'their Lord and their God'; – a triple evidence, first, of His Atonement; next of their own Resurrection unto glory; lastly, of His Divine Power to conduct them safely to it. Thus manifested as perfect God and perfect man, in the fulness of His sovereignty, and the immortality of His holiness, He ascended up on high to take possession of His kingdom. There He remains till the last day, 'Wonderful, Counsellor, The Mighty God, The Everlasting Father, The Prince of Peace.'[1]

Easter Day. Christ, a Quickening Spirit PPS II p. 143–4. 3 April, 1831

1 Isa 9,6

* The Readings of the Vigil precede the Mass

Easter Sunday

Acts 10, 34. 37–43; Col 3, 1–4; John 20, 1–9

'They have taken the Lord ...'

Or again: consider the account of His appearing to St. Mary Magdalene. While she stood at the sepulchre weeping He appeared, but she knew Him not. When He revealed Himself, He did not, indeed, at once vanish away, but He would not let her touch Him; as if, in another way, to show that His presence in His new kingdom was not to be one of sense. The two disciples were not allowed to *see* Him after recognizing Him, St. Mary Magdalene was not allowed to *touch* Him. But afterwards, St. Thomas *was* allowed both to see and touch; he had the full evidence of sense: but observe what our Lord says to him, 'Thomas, because thou hast seen Me, thou hast believed; blessed are they that have not seen, and yet have believed.' Faith is better than sight or touch.

The Spiritual Presence of Christ in the Church   PPS VI p. 133.   6 May, 1838

Second Sunday of Easter

Acts 2, 42–47; 1 Pet 1. 3–9; John 20, 19–31

'They had failed to understand that he must rise from the dead'

and so, in the history before us, the over-caution of St. Thomas has gained for us His promise of especial blessing on those who believe without having seen. I proceed to make some remarks on the nature of this believing temper, and why it is blessed.

It is scarcely necessary to observe, that what our Saviour says to Thomas so clearly and impressively, He has implied, in one way or other, all through His ministry; the blessedness of a mind that believes readily. His demand and trial of faith in the case of those who came for His miraculous aid, His praise of it where found, His sorrow where it was wanting, His warnings against hardness of heart; all are evidence of this. 'Verily I say unto you, I have not found so great faith, no, not in Israel.' 'Daughter, be of good comfort; thy faith hath made thee whole.' 'Thy faith hath saved thee; go in peace.' 'An evil and adulterous generation seeketh after a sign.' 'O fools, and slow of heart to believe all that the prophets have spoken.'[1]

St. Thomas. Faith without Sight   PPS II p. 16–17.   21 December, 1834

---

1   Matt. 8, 10. 9, 22. Luke 7, 50. Matt. 12, 39. Luke 24, 25.

Third Sunday of Easter

Acts 2, 14. 22–28; 1 Pet 1, 17–21; Luke 24, 13–35

'They recognised him in the Breaking of Bread'

Now observe what was the nature of His presence in the Church after His Resurrection. It was this, that He came and went as He pleased; that material substances, such as the fastened doors, were no impediments to His coming; and that when He was present His disciples did not, as a matter of course, know Him. St. Mark says He appeared to the two disciples who were going into the country, to Emmaus, *'in another form'*. St. Luke, who gives the account more at length, says, that while He talked with them their heart burned within them. And it is worth remarking, that the two disciples do not seem to have been conscious of this at the time, but on looking back, they recollected that as *having* been, which did not strike them while it *was*. 'Did not,' they say, *'did* not our heart burn within us, while He talked with us by the way, and while he opened to us the Scriptures?' But at the time, their hearts seem to have been holden (if we may use the expression) as well as their eyes. They were receiving impressions, but could not *realize* to themselves that they were receiving them; afterwards, however, they became aware of what had been. Let us observe, too, *when* it was that their eyes were opened; here we are suddenly introduced to the highest and most solemn Ordinance of the Gospel, for it was when He consecrated and brake the Bread that their eyes were opened. There is evidently a stress laid on this, for presently St. Luke sums up his account of the gracious occurrence with an allusion to it in particular; 'They told what things were done in the way, and how He was known of them in breaking of bread.' For so it was ordained, that Christ should not be both seen and known at once; first He was seen, then He was known. Only by faith is He known to be present; He is not recognized by sight. When He opened His disciples' eyes, He at once vanished. He removed His visible presence, and left but a memorial of Himself. He vanished from sight that He might be present in a sacrament; and in order to connect His visible presence with His presence invisible, He for one instant manifested Himself to their open eyes; manifested

Himself, if I may so speak, while He passed from His hiding-place of sight without knowledge, to that of knowledge without sight.

The Spiritual Presence of Christ in the Church   PPS VI p. 131−3.   6 May, 1838

Fourth Sunday of Easter

Acts 2, 14. 36–41; 1 Pet 2, 20–25; John 10, 1–10

'The Sheep follow because they know his voice'

What is here said about exercises of Reason, in order to believing? What is there not said of sympathetic feeling, of newness of spirit, of love? It was from lack of love towards Christ that the Jews discerned not in Him the Shepherd of their souls. 'Ye believe not, because ye are not of My sheep. My sheep hear My voice, and follow Me.' It was the regenerate nature sent down from the Father of Lights which drew up the disciples heavenward, – which made their affections go forth to meet the Bridegroom, and fixed those affections on Him, till they were as cords of love staying the heart upon the Eternal. 'All that the Father giveth Me, shall come to Me. No *man* can come unto Me, except the Father which hath sent Me draw him. It is written in the Prophets, And they shall be all taught of God. Every man, therefore, that hath heard and hath learned of the Father, cometh unto Me.' It is the new life, and not the natural reason which leads the soul to Christ. Does a child trust his parents because he has proved to himself that they are such, and that they are able and desirous to do him good, or from the instinct of affection? We *believe*, because we *love*. How plain a truth! What gain is it to be wise above that which is written? Why, O men, deface with your minute and arbitrary philosophy the simplicity, the reality, the glorious liberty of the inspired teaching? Is this your godly jealousy for Scripture? this your abhorrence of human additions?

It is the doctrine, then, of the text, that those who believe in Christ, believe because they know Him to be the Good Shepherd; and they know Him by His voice; and they know His voice, because they are His sheep; that they do not follow strangers and robbers, because they know not the voice of strangers: moreover, that they know and follow Christ, upon His loving them. 'I am come that they might have life. .... The hireling fleeth, because he is a hireling, and careth not for the sheep.' The divinely-enlightened mind sees in Christ the very Object whom it desires to love and worship, – the Object correlative of its own affections; and it trusts Him, or believes, from loving Him.

Love the Safeguard of Faith against Superstition   US p. 235–6.   21 May, 1839

Fifth Sunday of Easter

Acts 6, 1–7; 1 Pet 2, 4–9; John 14, 1–12

'The Way, the Truth and the Life'

My brethren, we say daily, 'We are His people, and the sheep of His pasture.' Again, we say, 'We have erred and strayed from Thy ways, like lost sheep': let us never forget these truths; let us never forget, on the one hand, that we are sinners; let us never forget, on the other hand, that Christ is our Guide and Guardian. He is 'the Way, the Truth, and the Life.' He is a light unto our ways and a lantern unto our paths. He is our Shepherd, and the sheep know His voice. If we are His sheep, we shall hear it, recognize it, and obey it. Let us beware of not following when he goes before: 'He goes before, and His sheep follow Him, for they know His voice.' Let us beware of receiving His grace in vain. When God called Samuel, he answered, 'Speak, Lord, for Thy servant heareth.' When Christ called St. Paul, he 'was not disobedient to the heavenly vision.'[1] Let us desire to know His voice; let us pray for the gift of watchful ears and a willing heart. He does not call all men in one way; He calls us each in His own way. To St. Peter He said, 'Follow thou Me;' of St. John, 'If I will that he tarry till I come, what is that to thee?' Nor is it always easy to know His voice. St. John knew it, and said, 'It is the Lord,' before St. Peter. Samuel did not know it till Eli told him. St. Paul asked, 'Who art Thou, Lord?' We are bid, 'try the spirits, whether they be of God.'[2] But whatever difficulty there be in knowing when Christ calls, and whither, yet at least let us look out for His call. Let us not be content with ourselves; let us not make our own hearts our home, or this world our home, or our friends our home; let us look out for a better country, that is, a heavenly. Let us look out for Him who alone can guide us to that better country; let us call heaven our home, and this life a pilgrimage; let us view ourselves, as sheep in the trackless desert, who, unless they follow the shepherd, will be sure to lose themselves, sure to fall in with the wolf. We are safe while we keep close to Him, and under His eye; but if we suffer Satan to gain an advantage over us, woe to us!

The Shepherd of our Souls   PPS VIII p. 241–3.   30 April, 1843

1   1 Sam 3, 10; Acts 26, 19
2   John 21, 19. 22; 21, 7; Acts 9, 5; 1 John 4, 1

Sixth Sunday of Easter

Acts 8, 5 – 8. 14 – 17; 1 Pet 3, 15 – 18; John 14, 15 – 21

'If you love me, keep my Commandments'

Turning from Him to ourselves, we find a short rule given us, 'If ye love Me, keep My commandments.' 'He that saith he abideth in Him, ought himself also so to walk, even as He walked.' 'If ye then be risen with Christ, seek those things which are above, where Christ sitteth on the right hand of God.'[1] This is all that is put upon us, difficult indeed to perform, but easy to understand; all that is put upon us, – and for this plain reason, because Christ has done everything else. He has freely chosen us, died for us, regenerated us, and now ever liveth for us; what remains? Simply that we should do as He has done to us, showing forth His glory by good works. Thus a correct (or as we commonly call it), an orthodox faith and an obedient life, is the whole duty of man. And so, most surely, it has ever been accounted. Look into the records of the early Church, or into the writings of our own revered bishops and teachers, and see whether this is not the sum total of religion, according to the symbols of it in which children are catechized, the Creed, the Lord's Prayer, and the Ten Commandments.

Easter Monday. Saving Knowledge PPS II p. 155 – 6. Jan/Feb 1835

---

1 John 14, 15; 1 John 2, 6; Col 3, 1

The Ascension of the Lord

Acts 1, 1–11; Eph 1, 17–23; Matt 28, 16–20

'All Authority has been given to me'

First, Christ's Ascension to the right hand of God is marvellous, because it is a sure token that heaven is a certain fixed place, and not a mere state. That bodily presence of the Saviour which the Apostles handled is not here; it is elsewhere, – it is in heaven. This contradicts the notions of cultivated and speculative minds, and humbles the reason. Philosophy considers it more rational to suppose that Almighty God, as being a Spirit, is in every place; and in no one place more than another. It would teach, if it dare, that heaven is a mere state of blessedness; but, to be consistent, it ought to go on to deny, with the ancient heretics, referred to by St. John, that 'Jesus Christ is come in the flesh,' and maintain that His presence on earth was a mere vision; for, certain it is, He who appeared on earth went up from the earth, and a cloud received Him out of His Apostles' sight. And here again an additional difficulty occurs, on minutely considering the subject. Whither did He go? beyond the sun? beyond the fixed stars? Did He traverse the immeasurable space which extends beyond them all? Again, what is meant by *ascending*? Philosophers will say there is no difference between *down* and *up*, as regards the sky; yet, whatever difficulties the word may occasion, we can hardly take upon us to decide that it is a mere popular expression, consistently with the reverence due to the Sacred Record.

Ascension Day. Mysteries in Religion   PPS II p. 207–8.   Nov/Dec 1834

Seventh Sunday of Easter

Acts 1, 12–14; 1 Pet 4, 13–16; John 17, 1–11

To bring down Heaven upon Earth

Our Saviour's words, spoken of the Apostles in the first instance, relate to the Church at large, – 'I pray not for the world, but for them which Thou hast given Me, for they are Thine.' In like manner St. Paul says that Christ came, not to convert the world, but 'to purify unto Himself a *peculiar people*, zealous of good works'; not to sanctify this evil world, but to 'deliver us *out of* this present evil world according to the will of God and our Father;[1] not to turn the whole earth into a heaven, but to bring down a heaven upon earth. This has been the real triumph of the Gospel, to raise those beyond themselves and beyond human nature, in whatever rank and condition of life, whose wills mysteriously co-operate with God's grace, who, while God visits them, really fear and really obey God, whatever be the unknown reason why one man obeys Him and another not. It has made men saints, and brought into existence specimens of faith and holiness, which without it are unknown and impossible.

The Visible Church for the Sake of the Elect   PPS IV p. 156.   20 November, 1836

---

1   John 17, 9; Tit. 2, 14; Gal. 1, 4

Pentecost Sunday

Acts 2, 1–11; 1 Cor 12, 3–7. 12–13; John 20, 19–23

'Receive the Holy Spirit'

In this respect, Christ's ministrations were above all that had ever been before Him, in bringing with them the gift of the Holy Ghost, that one gift, one, yet multiform, sevenfold in its operation, in which all spiritual blessedness is included. Accordingly, our Lord was solemnly anointed with the Holy Ghost Himself, as an initiation into His Ministerial office. He was manifested as receiving, that He might be believed on as giving. He was thus commissioned, according to the Prophet, 'to preach good tidings,' 'to heal the broken-hearted,' 'to give the oil of joy for mourning.' Therefore, in like manner, the Apostles also were anointed with the same heavenly gift for the same Ministerial office. 'He breathed on them, and saith unto them, Receive ye the Holy Ghost.' Such as was the consecration of the Master, such was that of the Disciples; and such as His, were the offices to which they were thereby admitted.

Christ is a Prophet, as authoritatively revealing the will of God and the Gospel of Grace. So also were the Apostles; 'He that heareth you, heareth Me; and he that despiseth you, despiseth Me: and he that despiseth Me, despiseth Him that sent Me'; 'He that despiseth, despiseth not man, but God, who hath also given unto us His Holy Spirit.'

Christ is a Priest, as forgiving sin, and imparting other needful divine gifts. The Apostles, too, had this power; 'Whose soever sins ye remit, they are remitted unto them; and whose soever sins ye retain, they are retained.'[1] 'Let a man so account of us as ... Stewards of the Mysteries of God.'

Christ is a King, as ruling the Church; and the Apostles rule it in His stead. 'I appoint unto you a Kingdom, as My Father hath appointed unto Me; that ye may eat and drink at My table in My Kingdom, and sit on thrones judging the twelve tribes of Israel.'[2]

St. Peter. The Christian Ministry   PPS II p. 302, 303–4.   14 December 1834

1   John 20, 21–23
2   1 Cor 4, 1; Gal 4, 14; 2 Cor 5, 20

The Most Holy Trinity

Exod 34, 4–6. 8–9; 2 Cor 13, 11–13; John 3, 16–18

God so loved the world that He gave his only Son

And this Mystery, which the Old Testament obscurely signifies, is in the New clearly declared; and it is this, – that the God of all, who is revealed in the Old Testament, is the Father of a Son from everlasting, called also His Word and Image, of His substance and partaker of all His perfections, and equal to Himself, yet without being separate from Him, but one with Him; and that from the Father and the Son proceeds eternally the Holy Spirit, who also is of one substance, Divinity, and majesty with Father and Son. Moreover we learn that the Son or Word is a Person, – that is, is to be spoken of as 'He,' not 'it,' and can be addressed; and that the Holy Ghost also is a Person. Thus God subsists in Three Persons, from everlasting to everlasting; first, God is the Father, next God is the Son, next God is the Holy Ghost; and the Father is not the Son, nor the Son the Holy Ghost, nor the Holy Ghost the Father. And God is Each of these Three, and nothing else; that is, he is either the Father, or the Son, or the Holy Ghost. Moreover, God is as wholly and entirely God in the Person of the Father, as though there were no Son and Spirit; as entirely in that of the Son, as though there were no Spirit and Father; as entirely in that of the Spirit, as though there were no Father and Son. And the Father is God, the Son God, and the Holy Ghost God, while there is but one God; and that without any inequality, because there is but One God, and He is without parts or degrees; though how it is that that same Adorable Essence, indivisible, and numerically One, should subsist perfectly and wholly in Each of Three Persons, no words of man can explain, nor earthly illustration typify.

The Mystery of the Holy Trinity PPS VI p. 357–8. Date not known

The Body and Blood of Christ

Deut 8, 2–3. 14–16; 1 Cor 10, 16–17; John 6, 51–58

'I am the Living Bread come down from Heaven'

You will see this more clearly by considering what our Saviour says about the blessed Sacrament of His Supper. He says He will give us His flesh to eat. How is this done? we do not know. He gives it under the outward symbols of bread and wine. But in what real sense is the consecrated bread His body? It is not told us, we may not inquire. We say indeed *spiritually, sacramentally, in a heavenly way*; but this is in order to impress on our minds religious, and not carnal notions of it. All we are concerned to know is, *the effect* upon us of partaking this blessed food. Now observe what He tells us about that. 'Except ye eat the flesh of the Son of man and drink His blood, ye have no life in you. Whoso eateth My flesh, and drinketh My blood, hath eternal life, and I will *raise him up at the last day.*' Now there is no distinction made here between soul and body. Christ's blessed Supper is food to us altogether, *whatever* we are, soul, body, and all. It is the seed of eternal life within us, the food of immortality, to 'preserve our body and soul unto everlasting life.'

The Resurrection of the Body   PPS I p. 274.   22 April, 1832

And now surely, my Brethren, we are come to the end of these wonders. He tore open the solid rock; He rose from the tomb; He ascended on high; He is far off from the earth; He is safe from profanation; and the soul and body, which He assumed, partake of course, as far as created nature allows, of the Sovereign Freedom and the Independence of Omnipotence. It is not so: He is indeed beyond the reach of suffering; but you anticipate, my Brethren, what I have yet to say. Is He then so enamoured of the prison, that He should purpose to revisit earth again, in order that, as far as possible, He may undergo it still? Does He set such a value on subjection to His creatures, that, before He goes away, on the very eve of His betrayal, He must actually make provision, after death, for perpetuating His captivity to the end of the world? My Brethren, the great truth is daily before our eyes: He has ordained the standing miracle of His Body and Blood under visible symbols, that He may secure thereby the standing mystery of Omnipotence in bonds.

He took bread, and blessed, and made it His Body; He took wine, and gave thanks, and made it His Blood; and He gave His priests the power to do what He had done.

Omnipotence in Bonds   OS p. 86−7.   1st after Epiphany, 1857

The Sacred Heart of Jesus

Deut 7, 6–11; 1 John 4, 7–16; Matt 11, 25–30

'Take my Yoke upon you and learn of me'

The exhortation, then, which our Saviour gives in today's Gospel, and of which St. Matthias's history reminds us, is at the present season most suitable. Our Saviour says, 'Come unto Me,' and then He adds, 'Take My yoke upon you, and learn of Me.' Thus He first calls us to Him, and next shows us the way. 'Come unto Me,' He says, 'and I will give you rest'; and then adds, 'Take My yoke upon you, and ye shall find rest for your souls.' He told the Apostles that they must come to Him, but did not at once tell them the way; He told them they must bear a yoke, but did not at once tell them what it was. St. Peter, in consequence, inquired about it on one occasion, and was bid to wait awhile, and he should know of it more plainly. Our Lord had said, 'Whither I go, thou canst not follow Me now, but thou shalt follow Me afterwards.' 'Ye shall seek Me,' He said, 'and whither I go ye cannot come.'[1]

Again, in another place, our Lord speaks more expressly; 'If any man will come after Me, let him deny himself, and take up his cross, and follow Me.'[2] Here we have the words of the text emphatically repeated. To come to Christ, is to come after Him; to take up our cross, is to take upon us His yoke; and though He calls this an easy yoke, yet it is easy because it is His yoke, and He makes it easy; still it does not cease to be a yoke, and it is troublesome and distressing, because it is a yoke.

The Yoke of Christ   PPS VII p. 104–5.   24 February, 1839

---

1   John 13, 36. 33
2   John 21, 18

Second Sunday of the year

Isa 49, 3. 5–6; 1 Cor 1, 1–3; John 1, 29–34

'He will baptise with the Holy Spirit'

Christ's religion has no fellowship with bare forms, and nowhere encourages mere outward observances. If, indeed, there be any who degrade Baptism into a mere ceremony, which has in it no spiritual promise, let such men look to it for themselves, and defend their practice of baptizing infants as they can. But for me, my brethren, I would put it before you as a true and plain pledge, without reserve, of God's grace given to the souls of those who receive it; not a mere form, but a real means and instrument of blessing verily and indeed received; and, as being such, I warn you to remember what a talent has been committed to you. There are very many persons who do not think of Baptism in this religious point of view; who are in no sense in the habit of blessing God for it, and praying Him for His further grace to profit by the privileges given them in it; who, when even they pray for grace, do not ground their hope of being heard and answered, on the promise of blessing in Baptism made to them; above all, who do not fear to sin after Baptism.

Infant Baptism   PPS VII p. 228.   15 June, 1828

Third Sunday of the Year

Isa 8, 23−9, 3; 1 Cor 1. 10−13. 17; Matt 4, 12−23

'Follow Me, and I will make you Fishers of Men'

For instance, we read of the Apostles, that 'Jesus, walking by the sea of Galilee, saw two brethren, Simon called Peter, and Andrew his brother, casting a net into the sea; for they were fishers. And He saith unto them, Follow Me, and I will make you fishers of men. *And* they *straightway* left their nets and followed Him.' Again; when He saw James and John with their father Zebedee, 'He *called* them; and they *immediately left the ship, and their father*, and *followed* Him.' And so of St. Matthew at the receipt of custom, 'He said unto him, Follow Me; and he left all, rose up, and followed Him.'

Again, we are told in St. John's Gospel, 'Jesus would go forth into Galilee, and findeth Philip, and saith unto Him, *Follow* Me.' Again, 'Philip findeth Nathanael,' and in like manner says to him, 'Come and see.' 'Jesus saw Nathanael coming unto Him, and saith of him, Behold an Israelite indeed, in whom is no guile.'

Divine Calls   PPS VIII p. 20−1.   27 October, 1839

Fourth Sunday of the Year

Zeph 2, 3. 3, 12–13; 1 Cor 1, 26–31; Matt 5, 1–12

'Happy are the Poor in Spirit'

The case is the same as regards poverty, which it is the fashion of the world to regard not only as the greatest of evils, but as the greatest *disgrace*. Men count it a disgrace, because it certainly does often arise from carelessness, sloth, imprudence, and other faults. But, in many cases, it is nothing else but the very state of life in which God has placed a man; but still, even then, it is equally despised by the world. Now if there is one thing clearly set forth in the Bible it is this, that 'Blessed are the poor.' Our Saviour was the great example of poverty; He was a poor man. St. Paul says, 'Ye know the grace of our Lord Jesus Christ, that, though He was rich, yet for your sakes He became poor, that ye through His poverty might be rich.'[1] Or consider St. Paul's very solemn language about the danger of wealth: 'The love of money is the root of all evil, which while some coveted after, they have erred from the faith, and pierced themselves through with many sorrows.'[2] Can we doubt that poverty is under the Gospel *better* than riches? I say *under* the Gospel, and *in* the regenerate, and *in* the true servants of God. Of course out of the Gospel, among the unregenerate, among the lovers of this world, it matters not whether one is rich or poor; a man is any how unjustified, and there is no better or worse in his outward circumstances. But, I say, *in Christ* the poor is in a more blessed lot than the wealthy. Ever since the Eternal Son of God was born in a stable, and had not a place to lay His head, and died an outcast and as a malefactor, heaven has been won by poverty, by disgrace, and by suffering. Not by these things in themselves, but by faith working in and through them.

The Weapons of Saints　PPS VI p. 323–4.　29 October, 1837

1　2 Cor 8, 9
2　1 Tim 6, 10

Fifth Sunday of the Year

Isa 58, 7–10; 1 Cor 2, 1–5; Matt 5, 13–16

'You are the Light of the World'

Our Saviour gives us a command, in this passage of His Sermon on the Mount, to manifest our religious profession before all men. 'Ye are the light of the world,' He says to His disciples; 'A city that is set on a hill cannot be hid. Neither do men light a candle and put it under a bushel, but on a candlestick; and it giveth light unto all that are in the house. Let your light so shine before men, that they may see your good works, and glorify your Father which is in heaven.' Yet presently He says, 'When thou doest alms ... when thou prayest ... when ye fast ... appear not unto men ... but unto thy Father which is in secret.'[1] How are these commands to be reconciled? how are we at once to *profess* ourselves Christians, and yet hide our Christian words, deeds, and self-denials?

I will now attempt to answer this question; that is, to explain how we may be witnesses to the world for God, and yet without pretension, or affectation, or rude and indecent ostentation.

Now, first, much might be said on that mode of witnessing Christ which consists in conforming to His Church. He who simply did what the Church bids him do (if he did no more), would witness a good confession to the world, and one which cannot be hid; and at the same time, with very little, if any, personal display. He does only what he is told to do; he takes no responsibility on himself. The Apostles and Martyrs who founded the Church, the Saints in all ages who have adorned it, the Heads of it now alive, all these take from him the weight of his profession, and bear the blame (so to call it) of seeming ostentations.

Profession without Ostentation   PPS I p. 152–3.   6 November, 1831

---

1   Matt 6, 2–18

Sixth Sunday of the Year

Sir 15, 15–20; 1 Cor 2, 6–10; Matt 5, 17–37

'Keeping the Commandments'

These are a few out of a multitude of traits which mark an easy religion, – the religion of the world; which would cast in its lot with Christian truth, were not that truth so very strict, and quarrels with it and its upholders, not as if it were not good and right, but because it is so unbending, – because it will not suit itself to times and emergencies, and to the private and occasional likings and tastes of individuals. This is the kind of religion which St. Paul virtually warns us against, as often as he speaks of the Gospel as really being a law and a servitude. He indeed glories in its being such; for, as the happiness of all creatures lies in their performing their parts well, where God has placed them, so man's greatest good lies in obedience to God's law and in imitation of God's perfections. But the Apostle knew that the world would not think so, and therefore he insists on it. Therefore it is that he insists on the necessity of Christians '*fulfilling* the righteousness of the law'; fulfilling it, because till we aim at complete, unreserved obedience in all things, we are not really Christians at all. Hence St. James says, 'Whosoever shall keep the whole law, and yet offend in one point, he is guilty of all.' And our Saviour assures us that 'Whosoever shall break one of these least commandments, and shall teach men so, he shall be called least in the kingdom of heaven'; and that 'Except our righteousness shall exceed the righteousness of the Scribes and Pharisees,' which was thus partial and circumscribed, 'we shall in no case enter into the kingdom of heaven.'[1]

The Strictness of the Law of Christ PPS IV p. 11–12. 9 July, 1837

---

[1] Rom 8, 4; Jas 2, 10; Matt 5, 19. 20

Seventh Sunday of the Year

Lev 19, 1–2, 17–18; 1 Cor 3, 16–23; Matt 5, 38–48

'Love your Enemies . . . '

It is scarcely supposable that one should have so little generosity as to refuse forgiveness to one who confessed himself wrong and asked to be forgiven.

But when he does not ask to be forgiven; if he persists in opposition and injury, and goes on doing harm, and takes a wrong course. Yet this commanded too. The Lord's Prayer – Matt. 6. 14–15, Mark 11, 25–26, Rom 12. 18–20.

Or again, supposing he does not do so, asks to make it up, still there may be, you may say, such difficulties as these: I may wish to keep at a distance, for:

(1) *E.g.* I cannot trust him; he is a dangerous man.

(2) He is likely to do me spiritual harm.

(3) The sight of him is a temptation, an irritation to me; we shall be best friends at a distance.

(4) I shall be a hypocrite if I make it up, for I don't like his doings.

(5) I ought to protest against him.

ANSWER. – 'If you *in your hearts forgive* not every one his brother'. Matt. 18, 35. You must love him. Col. 3, 12–13; Matt. 5, 44–47.

OBJECTION. – 'But I do not like him. How can I love him?' *This* is a fundamental difficulty.

ANSWER. – Can you pray that you may meet him and love him in heaven? You and he are both far from what you should be; and each has to *change*. Look on the *best* part of his character – learn sympathy with him. Think how he suffers. Purgatory useful for this – to bring you and him nearer to each other.

Forgiveness of Injuries　SN 244–6.　13 October, 1872

We are bidden lend and give, asking for nothing again; revenge not ourselves; give our cloak when our coat is taken; offer the left cheek when the right is smitten; suffer without complaint; account persons better than they are; keep from bitter words; pray only when others would be impatient to act; deny ourselves for the sake of others; live contented with what we are; preserve an ignorance of sin and of the world: what is all this, but a character of mind which the world scorns and ridicules even more than it hates? a character which seems to court insult, because it endures it?

PPS VII p. 111.   24 February, 1839

Eighth Sunday of the Year

Isa 49, 14–15; 1 Cor 4, 1–5; Matt 6, 24–34

Divine Providence

'But this I say, brethren, the time is short.' What matters it what we eat, what we drink, how we are clothed, where we lodge, what is thought of us, what becomes of us, since we are not at home? It is felt every day, even as regards this world, that when we leave home for a while we are unsettled. This, then, is the kind of feeling which a belief in Christ's coming will create within us. It is not worth while establishing ourselves here; it is not worth while spending time and thought on such an object. We shall hardly have got settled when we shall have to move.

This being apparently the general drift of the passage, let us next enter into the particular portions of it.

'Be careful for nothing,' he says, or, as St. Peter, 'casting all your care upon Him,' or, as He Himself, 'Take no thought' or care 'for the morrow, for the morrow will take thought for the things of itself.'[1] This of course is the state of mind which is directly consequent on the belief, that 'the Lord is at hand.' Who would care for any loss or gain to-day, if he knew for certain that Christ would show Himself to-morrow? no one. Well, then, the true Christian feels as he would feel, did he know for certain that Christ would be here to-morrow. For he knows for certain, that at least Christ will come to him when he dies; and faith anticipates his death, and makes it just as if that distant day, if it *be* distant, were past and over. One time or another Christ will come, for certain: and when He once *has* come, it matters not what length of time there was before He came; – however long that period may be, it has an end. Judgment is coming, whether it comes sooner or later, and the Christian realizes that it is coming; that is, time does not enter into his calculation, or interfere with his view of things. When men expect to carry out their plans and projects, then they care for them; when they know these will come to nought, they give them over, or become indifferent to them.

Equanimity   PPS V p. 62–3.   22 December, 1839

1   1 Peter 5, 7. Matt. 6, 34.

Ninth Sunday of the Year

Deut 11, 18. 26−28. 32; Rom 3, 21−25. 28; Matt 7, 21−27

'God, the Foundation of Faith'

... in our Saviour's first parable, who is he who builds his house upon a rock? not he who has faith merely, but he, who having doubtless faith to begin the work, has faith also strong enough to perfect it; who 'heareth *and doeth.*'

The State of Salvation   PPS V p. 185.   18 March, 1838

He who has begun a good work in you, will perfect it; He who has chosen you, will be faithful to you; put your cause into His hand, wait upon Him, and you will surely persevere. What good work will you ever begin, if you bargain first to see the end of it? If you wish to do all at once, you will do nothing; he has done half the work, who has begun it well; you will not gain your Lord's praise at the final reckoning by hiding His talent. No; when he brings you from error to truth, He will have done the more difficult work (if aught is difficult to Him), and surely He will preserve you from returning from truth to error. Take the experience of those who have gone before you in the same course; they had many fears that their faith would fail them, before taking the great step, but those fears vanished on their taking it; they had fears, before they received the grace of faith, lest, after receiving it, they should lose it again, but no fears (except on the ground of their general frailness) after it was actually given them.

Faith and Doubt   Mix p. 232−3 (Discourse 11)   1849

Tenth Sunday of the Year

Hos 6, 3–6; Rom 4, 18–25; Matt 9, 9–13

He who begins with faith

Faith is the element of all perfection; he who begins with faith, will end in unspotted and entire holiness. It is the earnest of a great deal more than itself, and therefore is allowed, in God's consideration, to stand for, to be a pledge of, to be taken in advance for that, which it for certain will end in. He who believes has not yet perfect righteousness and unblameableness, but he has the first fruits of it. And all through a man's life, whether his righteous deeds be more or less, or his righteousness of heart more or less, his faith is something quite distinct from anything he had in a state of nature, and though it does not satisfy the requirements of God's law, yet since it tends to perfection, it is mercifully taken as perfection. 'Abraham believed God, and it was counted to him for righteousness,' because God, who sees the end from the beginning, knew it would end in perfect and unblemished righteousness. And in like manner to us 'it shall be imputed, if we believe on Him that raised up Jesus our Lord from the dead, who was delivered for our offences, and raised again for our justification.'[1]

They desired to be righteous; it was well; but Christ alone was 'the end of the Law for righteousness to every one that believed.' They desired to fulfil the Law; well then, let them seek 'the Law of the Spirit of life,' whereby 'the righteousness of the Law might be fulfilled in them.' They desired the reward of righteousness: be it so; let them then 'wait through the Spirit for the hope of righteousness by faith.'[2] But they were too proud to confess that they had anything to learn, that they had to begin again, to submit to be taught, to believe in Him they had crucified, to come suppliantly for the gift of the Spirit. They refused the true righteousness which God had provided, thinking they were righteous as they were, and that they could be saved in the flesh. Hence St. Paul says, 'They, being ignorant of God's righteousness, and going about to establish their own righteousness, have not submitted themselves unto the righteousness of God.'[3]

The Law of the Spirit   PPS V p. 159, 161.   12 January, 1840

1   Rom 4, 24. 25
2   Gal 5.5
3   Rom 10, 3

Eleventh Sunday of the Year

Exod 19, 2–6; Rom 5, 6–11; Matt 9, 36–10, 8

He specially chose Twelve ...

Remember, too, this further reason why the witnesses of the Resurrection were few in number; viz. because they were on the side of *Truth*. If the witnesses were to be such as really loved and obeyed the Truth, there *could not* be many chosen. Christ's cause was the cause of light and religion, therefore His advocates and ministers were necessarily few. It is an old proverb (which even the heathen admitted), that 'the many are bad.' Christ did not confide His Gospel to the many; had He done so, we may even say, that it would have been at first sight a presumption against its coming from God. What was the chief work of His whole ministry, but that of choosing and separating *from* the multitude those who should be fit recipients of His Truth? As He went the round of the country again and again, through Galilee and Judea, He tried the spirits of men the while; and rejecting the baser sort who 'honoured Him with their lips while their hearts were far from Him,' He specially chose twelve. The many He put aside for a while as an adulterous and sinful generation, intending to make one last experiment on the mass when the Spirit should come. But His twelve He brought near to Himself at once, and taught them. Then He sifted them, and one fell away; the eleven escaped as though by fire. *For* these eleven especially He rose again; He visited *them* and taught *them* for forty days; for in *them* He saw the fruit of the 'travail of His soul and was satisfied'; in them 'He saw His seed, He prolonged His days, and the pleasure of the Lord prospered in His hand.' These were His witnesses, for they had the love of the Truth in their hearts. 'I have chosen you,' He says to them, 'and ordained you that ye should go and bring forth fruit, and that your fruit should remain.'[1]

Witnesses of the Resurrection   PPS I p. 288–9.   24 April, 1831

---

1   John 15, 16

Twelfth Sunday of the Year

Jer 20, 10–13; Rom 5, 12–15; Matt 10, 26–33

'Do not be afraid of those who kill the body'

For what is this kingdom as I have already described it? a universal empire without earthly arms; temporal pretensions without temporal sanctions; a claim to rule without the power to enforce; a continual tendency to acquire with a continual exposure to be dispossessed; greatness of mind with weakness of body. What will be the fortunes of such an empire in the world? persecution; persecution is the token of the Church; persecution is the note of the Church, perhaps the most abiding note of all. The world is strong: men of the world have arms of the world; they have swords, they have armies, they have prisons, they have chains, they have wild passions. The Church has none of these, and yet it claims a right to rule, direct, rebuke, exhort, denounce, condemn. It claims the obedience of the powerful; it confronts the haughty; it places itself across the path of the wilful; it undertakes the defence of the poor; it accepts the gifts of the world, and becomes involved in their stewardship; and yet it is at the mercy of these said powerful, haughty, and wilful men, to ill-treat and to spoil. Is not this too great a temptation for sinful nature to resist? Can it be otherwise, but that a kingdom which claims so much, which professes so much, yet can resist so little, which irritates the world's pride, which inflames its cupidity, which interferes with its purposes, which terrifies its conscience, yet does nothing in its defence but threaten; which deals with unseen ill and unseen good, whose only arms are what an unbelieving world calls priest-craft – is it not certain that such a kingdom will be the prey and sport of the world?

Condition of the Members of the Christian Empire   SD p. 260–1.   31 May, 1840

Thirteenth Sunday of the Year

2 Kgs 4, 8–11. 14–16; Rom 6, 3–4. 8–11; Matt 10, 37–42

'Anyone who welcomes you, welcomes me'

This is a great Scripture truth, which in this busy and sanguine day needs insisting upon. There are in every age a certain number of souls in the world, known to God, unknown to us, who will obey the Truth when offered to them, whatever be the mysterious reason that they do and others do not. These we must contemplate, for these we must labour, these are God's special care, for these are all things; of these and among these we must pray to be, and our friends with us, at the Last Day. They are the true Church, ever increasing in number, ever gathering in, as time goes on; with them lies the Communion of Saints; they have power with God; they are His armies who follow the Lamb, who overcome princes of the earth, and who shall hereafter judge Angels. These are that multitude which took its beginning in St. Paul's day, for which he laboured, having his portion in it himself; for which we in our day must labour too, that, if so be, we too may have a place in it: according to the text, 'He that receiveth a prophet in the name of a prophet shall receive a prophet's reward; and he that receiveth a righteous man in the name of a righteous man shall receive a righteous man's reward. And whosoever shall give to drink unto one of these little ones a cup of cold water only in the name of a disciple, verily I say unto you, he shall in no wise lose his reward.'

The Visible Church for the Sake of the Elect   PPS IV p. 153–4.
20 November, 1836

Fourteenth Sunday of the Year

Zech 9, 9–10; Rom 8, 9. 11–13; Matt 11, 25–30

There is but one Cross and one character of mind formed by it

Where Christ is put on, St. Paul tells us, there is neither Jew nor Greek, bond nor free, male nor female, but all are one in Christ Jesus.[1] What Lazarus is, that must Dives become; what Apostles were, that must each of us be. The high in this world think it suitable in them to show a certain pride and self-confidence; the wealthy claim deference on account of their wealth; kings and princes think themselves above instruction from any; men in the middle ranks consider it enough to be decent and respectable, and deem sanctity superfluous in them; the poor think to be saved by their poverty; – but to one and all Christ speaks, 'Come unto Me,' 'Learn of Me.' There is but one Cross and one character of mind formed by it; and nothing can be further from it than those tempers and dispositions in which the greater part of men called Christians live.

The Yoke of Christ   PPS VII p. 114–5.   24 February, 1839

---

1   Gal 3, 28

Fifteenth Sunday of the Year

Isa 55, 10–11; Rom 8, 18–23; Matt 13, 1–23

The Sower

Again, in the parable of the Sower, the simple question considered is, who they are who profit by what they have received; what a Christian has to do is represented as a *work*, a process which has a beginning, middle, and end; a consistent course of obedience, not a state in which we have done nothing more at the end of our lives than at the beginning, except sin the oftener, according to its length. In that parable one man is said not to admit the good seed; a second admits it, but its root withers; a third goes further, the seed strikes root, and shoots upwards, but its leaves and blossoms get entangled and overlaid with thorns. The fourth takes root, shoots upwards, and does more, bears fruit to perfection. This then is the Christian's great aim, viz. not to come short after grace given him.

The State of Salvation   PPS V p. 185.   18 March, 1838

In the parable of the Sower, which has formed the Gospel for this day, we have set before us four descriptions of men, all of whom receive the word of God. The sower sows first on the hard ground or road, then on the shallow earth or rock, then on a ground where other seeds were sown, and lastly on really good, rich, well-prepared soil. By the sower is meant the preacher; and by the seed the word preached; and by the rock, the road, the preoccupied ground, and the good soil are meant four different states of mind of those who hear the word. Now, here we have a picture laid out before us which will, through God's mercy, provide us with a fitting subject of thought this evening.

First let us consider the case of the hard ground and the seed that was sown there — 'some fell by the road and was trodden down and the birds of the heaven ate it up ...

You will observe that, in the parable, not only did the fowls carry off the word of life, but the foot of the passer-by trampled it.

... Exhort one another every day, whilst it is called today, lest any be hardened by the deceitfulness of sin' (Heb. 3.13). When the heart is hard, the birds take away the divine seeds. They do not bring it back; it goes for ever. Make the most of the precious time. Delay not — many a soul has been damned by delay. God's opportunities do not wait; they come and they go. The word of life waits not — if it is not appropriated by you, the devil will appropriate. He delays not, but has his eyes wide always, and is ready to pounce down and carry off the gift which you delay to use.

The Calls of Grace CS p. 43, 48, 52, 27 February, 1848, St Chad's, Birmingham

Sixteenth Sunday of the Year

Wisd 12, 13. 16–19; Rom 8, 26–27; Matt 13, 24–43

The Seed that was sown

Let us then endeavour, by His grace, rightly to understand where we stand, and what He is towards us; most tender and pitiful, yet, for all His pity, not passing by the breadth of a single hair the eternal lines of truth, holiness, and justice; He who can condemn to the woe everlasting, though He weeps and laments beforehand, and who, when once the sentence of condemnation has gone forth, will wipe out altogether the remembrance of us, 'and know us not.' The tares were 'bound in bundles' for the burning, indiscriminately, promiscuously, contemptuously. 'Let us then fear, lest a promise being left us of entering into His rest, any of us should seem to come short of it.'

A Particular Providence as Revealed in the Gospel   PPS III p. 127.   5 April, 1835

Moreover, the mustard-seed, small and vile though it be, was destined to spread and thrive; to thrive in spite of all the world's power. Here is a distinct provocation. What so irritating, so mortifying to the proud, who are conscious that they are in high place in the world, and have great worldly power or influence, the world's arms, the world's homage, as to find a despised doctrine 'grow and multiply' in spite of them, and by means which they cannot investigate, by powers which they cannot analyze? Such was the nature of the Church's triumph over heathenism; and what the counter triumph over heathenism would be over the Church, was plain before the event. 'It shall bruise thy head, and thou shalt bruise His heel.'[1] The Church made progress, and the world persecuted.

Condition of the Members of the Christian Empire   SD p. 261–2.   31 May, 1840

1   Gen 3, 15

Seventeenth Sunday of the Year

1 Kgs 3, 5. 7–12; Rom 8, 28–30; Matt 13, 44–52

... *Like a Net cast into the Sea*

That Scripture then speaks of the Kingdom of Christ as not an earthly kingdom, not supported by stength of arm, or force of mind, or any other faculty or gift of the natural man, is plain. But now let us consider some objections to which the circumstances of its actual history and condition give rise.

And first, it may be said that the event has not fulfilled the prophecies, in this very respect in which I have been speaking of them; that the kingdom has indeed been large and powerful, but it has not ruled according to justice and truth; that at times it has had very wicked men among its rulers, and that great corruptions, religious and moral, have been found in it; and that, as has sometimes been said, worse crimes have been perpetrated under colour of religion than in any other way. But this may be granted in the argument, and yet the Scripture account of the Church remains uncompromised. That there have been things that offend, and those that commit iniquity, in Christ's kingdom, in great abundance, is true indeed; but of this we are forewarned in Scripture itself. 'The kingdom of heaven,' says our Lord, 'is like unto a net that was cast into the sea, and gathered of *every kind*.' Nor does the one truth interfere with the other. It is true there have been 'many called and few chosen' in this kingdom; yet it is true also, that it is a kingdom of righteousness, for this reason, because it is a kingdom *founded, based* in righteousness.

But Christ's kingdom was of another sort. It was destined to be powerful and wide-spreading above other kingdoms; it was to be the abode of proud, covetous, ambitious, sensual hearts; it was to look like the kingdoms of this world, first, because of its wealth and power; next, because there were many among its subjects who sought these things. But this is the indelible distinction between it and all other kingdoms, that they spring from evil, and depend on evil; they have their life and strength in bold deeds and bad principles: but that the life of the Church lies, not in inflicting evil, but in receiving it; not in doing, but in suffering; in all those things which the world despises, as being fitter in themselves to pull down an empire than to build it up; in patience, in simplicity, in innocence, in concession, in passiveness, in resignation.

Sanctity the Token of the Christian Empire   SD p. 241, 243–4.   4 December, 1842

The Church is a collection of souls, brought together in one by God's secret grace, though that grace comes to them through visible instruments, and unites them to a visible hierarchy. What is seen, is not the whole of the Church, but the visible part of it.

Secret Power of Divine Grace   OS p. 57.   28th after Pentecost, 1856

Eighteenth Sunday of the Year

Isa 55, 1–3; Rom 8, 35. 37–39; Matt 14, 13–21

The Miracle of the Loaves

What, in short, is *meant* by multiplying the loaves? As to Christ's other miracles, they are, it may be said, intelligible though supernatural. We do not know *how* a blind man's eyes are opened, or the dead raised; but we know what is *meant* by saying that the blind saw, or the dead arose: but what *is meant* by saying that the loaves fed five thousand persons? Such then is the objection which may be brought against the miracle of the loaves; and let it be observed, it is just such as this which is urged against the mystery of Christ's Presence in Holy Communion. If the marvellousness of the miracle of the loaves is no real objection to its truth, neither is the marvellousness of the Eucharistic presence any real difficulty in our believing that gift.

And as if still more closely to connect this Holy Sacrament with the miracle of the Loaves, and to make the latter interpret the former, our Lord, as I have observed, wrought the miracle of the loaves by means of the same outward acts, which he observed in the mystery of His Supper, and which His Apostles have carefully recorded as the appointed means of consecrating it. St. John says, He *took* the loaves, and when *He had given thanks*, He *distributed* to the disciples.'

The Eucharistic Presence   SD p. 317.   28 November, 1841

Nineteenth Sunday of the Year

1 Kgs 19, 9. 11 – 13; Rom 9, 1 – 5; Matt 14, 22 – 33

The Venture of Faith

ST. PETER'S faith was one of his characteristic graces. It was ardent, keen, watchful, and prompt. It dispensed with argument, calculation, deliberation, and delay, whenever it heard the voice of its Lord and Saviour: and it heard that voice even when its accents were low, or when it was unaided by the testimony of the other senses. When Christ appeared walking on the sea, and said, 'It is I,' Peter answered Him, and said, 'Lord, if it be Thou, bid me come unto Thee on the water.' When Christ asked His disciples who He was, 'Simon Peter answered and said,' as we read in the Gospel for this day, 'Thou art the Christ, the Son of the Living God,' and obtained our Lord's blessing for such clear and ready Faith. At another time, when Christ asked the Twelve whether they would leave Him as others did, St. Peter said, 'Lord, to whom shall we go? Thou hast the words of eternal life; and we believe and are sure that Thou art the Christ, the Son of the Living God.' And after the Resurrection, when he heard from St. John that it was Christ who stood on the shore, he sprang out of the boat in which he was fishing, and cast himself into the sea, in his impatience to come near Him. Other instances of his faith might be mentioned. If ever Faith forgot self, and was occupied with its Great Object, it was the faith of Peter. If in any one Faith appears in contrast with what we commonly understand by Reason, and with Evidence, it so appears in the instance of Peter. When he reasoned, it was at times when Faith was lacking. 'When he saw the wind boisterous, he was afraid'; and Christ in consequence called him, 'Thou of little faith.' When He had asked, 'Who touched Me?' Peter and others reasoned, 'Master,' said they, 'the multitude throng Thee, and press Thee, and sayest Thou, Who touched Me?' And in like manner, when Christ said that he should one day follow Him in the way of suffering, 'Peter said unto Him, Lord, *why* cannot I follow Thee now?' – and we know how his faith gave way soon afterwards.

Implicit and Explicit Reason US p. 251 – 2. 29 June, 1840

Twentieth Sunday of the Year

Isa 56, 1. 6−7; Rom 11, 13−15. 29−32; Matt 15, 21−28

The Reward of Faith

Now, first, I think it will be granted by any one who knows Scripture well, that the doctrine laid down by our Lord on the occasion in question, He had expressed on other occasions and in other ways. For instance, He said, 'Unless you see signs and wonders, you believe not.' Elsewhere we read, 'He wrought not many miracles then, because of their unbelief.' In these passages He implies that hardness of belief is a fault. Elsewhere He praises easiness of belief. For instance, 'O woman, great is thy faith.' 'Amen, I say to you, I have not found so great faith in Israel.' 'Be of good heart, daughter, thy faith hath made thee whole.' 'Thy faith hath made thee safe, go in peace.' 'If thou canst believe, all things are possible to him that believeth.' I might quote many other passages to the same effect, from the Gospels, the Acts of the Apostles, and St. Paul's Epistles.

Now these passages cannot mean that faith is against reason, or that reason does not ordinarily precede faith, for this is a doctrine quite contrary to Revelation, but I think I shall not be wrong in understanding them thus, − that with good dispositions, faith is easy; and that without good dispositions, faith is *not* easy; and that those who were praised for their faith, were such as had already the good dispositions, and that those who were blamed for their unbelief, were such as were wanting in this respect, and would have believed, or believed sooner, had they possessed the necessary dispositions for believing, or a greater share of them. This is the point I am going to insist on: I am led to it by the Baptist's especial office of 'preparing the way of the Lord'; for by that preparation is meant the creating in the hearts of his hearers the dispositions necessary for faith. And I consider that the same truth is implied in the glorious hymn of the Angels upon Christmas night; for to whom was the Prince of Peace to come? They sang, 'Glory to God in the highest, and on earth *peace* to *men of good will.*' By 'good will' is meant, 'good disposition'; the peace of the Gospel, the full gifts of the knowledge, and of the power, and of the consolation of Christian Redemption, were to be the reward of men of *good dispositions. They* were the men to whom the Infant Saviour came; *they* were those in whom His grace would find its fruit and recompense; *they* were those, who, by congruous merit, would be led on, as the Evangelist says, to '*believe* in His Name,' and 'to be born, not of blood, nor of the will of the flesh, nor of the will of man, but of God.'[1]

Dispositions for Faith   OS p. 62–3.   4th after Advent, 1856. St Chad's, Birmingham

---

1   John 1, 13

Twenty-first Sunday of the Year

Isa 22, 19–23; Rom 11, 33–36; Matt 16, 13–20

The Rock on which the Church is founded

Too many persons at this day, – in spite of what they see before them, in spite of what they read in history, – too many persons forget, or deny, or do not know, that Christ has set up a kingdom in the world. In spite of the prophecies, in spite of the Gospels and Epistles, in spite of their eyes and their ears, – whether it be their sin or their misfortune, so it is, – they do not obey Him in that way in which it is His will that He should be obeyed. They do not obey Him in His Kingdom; they think to be His people, without being His subjects. They determine to serve Him in their own way; and though He has formed His chosen into one body, they think to separate from that body, yet to remain in the number of the chosen.

Far different in the doctrine suggested to us by the text. In St. Peter, who is there made the rock on which the Church is founded, we see, as in a type, its unity, stability, and permanence. It is set up in one name, not in many, to show that it is one; and that name is Peter, to show that it will last, or, as the Divine Speaker proceeds, that 'the gates of hell shall not prevail against it.' In like manner St. Paul calls it 'the pillar and ground of the truth.'[1]

The Unity of the Church   PPS VII p. 230–1.   November, 1829
cf. The Feast of St. Peter and St. Paul

---

1   1 Tim 3,15

Twenty-second Sunday of the Year

Jer 20, 7−9; Rom 12, 1−2; Matt 16, 21−27

The Scandal of the Cross

It may be granted, then, that the doctrine of the Cross is not on the surface of the world. The surface of things is bright only, and the Cross is sorrowful; it is a hidden doctrine; it lies under a veil; it at first sight startles us, and we are tempted to revolt from it. Like St. Peter, we cry out, 'Be it far from Thee, Lord; this shall not be unto Thee.'[1] And yet it is a true doctrine; for truth is not on the surface of things, but in the depths.

And thus 'Jesus Christ and He crucified' is, as the Apostle tells us, 'a hidden wisdom'; − hidden in the world, which seems at first sight to speak a far other doctrine, − and hidden in the faithful soul, which to persons at a distance, or to chance beholders, seems to be living but an ordinary life, while really it is in secret holding communion with Him who was 'manifested in the flesh,' 'crucified through weakness,' 'justified in the Spirit, seen of Angels, and received up into glory.'[1]

The Cross of Christ the Measure of the World   PPS VI p. 88−9.   9 April, 1841

---

1   1 Tim 3, 16

We have in the Gospel for this day what, I suppose, has raised the wonder of most readers of the New Testament. I mean the slowness of the disciples to take in the notion that our Lord was to suffer on the Cross. It can only be accounted for by the circumstance that a contrary opinion had strong possession of their minds – what we call a strong prejudice against the truth, in their case an honest religious prejudice, the prejudice of honest religious minds, but still a deep and violent prejudice. When our Lord first declared it, St Peter said, 'Be it far from Thee, Lord, this shall not happen to Thee.' He spoke so strongly that the Holy Evangelist says that he 'took our Lord and began to rebuke Him'. He did it out of reverence and love, as the occasion of it shows, but still that he spoke with warmth, with vehemence, is evident from the expression. Think then how deep his prejudice must have been.

Prejudice and Faith   CS p. 55.   5 March, 1848. St Chad's, Birmingham

Twenty-third Sunday of the Year

Ezek 33, 7–9; Rom 13, 8–10; Matt 18, 15–20

Obedience to the Church

Accordingly, when the Christians of Corinth went into parties, and set up forms of doctrine of their own and neglected St. Paul their Apostle, what did he say? did he *forbear* to forbid them? no, he forbade them. And he gave this reason; 'What?' he said, 'came the word of God out from you?'[1] that is, did the word of God originate with you? And in like manner we may say to those who set up a distinct sect or communion for themselves, Where did you get your knowledge of the truth? You may think the word of God came out from you, but really it came to you *from us*; nor have you received what you teach, as far as it is true, except through that Church which you oppose. That Church made you what you are, as far as you are Christian; and the Church that made you has a right to rule you, and to protest against you when you will not be ruled; she has a right to bid you follow her, and to claim jurisdiction over you, for you are hers; whereas the man in the text who cast out devils had not received the power through the Apostles, and therefore the Apostles had no claim on him to submit to them.

Afterwards, however, the Apostles were the sole channels of grace; and as they were the sole grace-givers under Christ, so they were the sole governors, under Him, of all Christian people; and as they transmitted life, so they claimed obedience. For instance, St. John the Baptist's disciples were believers, religious men, and in God's favour; but, when once the Church was set up, they were obliged to submit to the Church, and to leave the sect, though divinely founded, to which they belonged.

The Fellowship of the Apostles   PPS VI p. 197–8.   5 October, 1839

---

1   1 Cor. 14, 36

Twenty-fourth Sunday of the Year

Sir 27, 30–28, 9; Rom 14, 7–9; Matt 18, 21–35

Repaying our Talents

For surely it is not enough to avoid evil in order to attain to heaven, – we must follow after good. What, then, is their danger? – That of the unprofitable servant who hid his lord's money. As far removed as that slothful servant was from those who traded with their talents, in his state and in his destiny, so far separate from one another are two classes of Christians who live together here as brethren, – the one class is using grace, the other neglecting it; one is making progress, the other sitting still; one is working for a reward, the other is idle and worthless.

This view of things should ever be borne in mind when we speak of the state of grace. There are different degrees in which we may stand in God's favour; we may be rising or sinking in His favour; we may not have forfeited it, yet we may not be securing it; we may be safe for the present, but have a dangerous prospect before us. We may be more or less 'hypocrites,' 'slothful,' 'unprofitable,' and yet our day of grace not be passed. We may still have the remains of our new nature lingering on us, the influences of grace present with us, and the power of amendment and conversion within us. We may still have talents which we may put to account, and gifts which we may stir up. We may not be cast out of our state of justification, and yet may be destitute of that love of God, love of God's truth, love of holiness, love of active and generous obedience, that honest surrender of self, which alone will secure to us hereafter the blessed words, 'Well done, good and faithful servant; enter thou into the joy of thy Lord.'[1]

The Power of the Will   PPS V p. 342–3.   1 March, 1840

---

1   Matt 25, 21

Twenty-fifth Sunday of the Year

Isa 55, 6–9; Phil 1, 20–24. 27; Matt 20, 1–16

The Workers in the Vineyard

O may we ever bear in mind that we are not sent into this world to stand all the day idle, but to go forth to our work and to our labour until the evening! *Until* the evening, not *in* the evening only of life, but serving God from our youth, and not waiting till our years fail us. Until the *evening*, not in the day-time only, lest we begin to run well, but fall away before our course is ended. Let us 'give glory to the Lord our God, before He cause darkness, and before our feet stumble upon the dark mountains';[1] and, having turned to Him, let us see that our goodness be not 'as the morning cloud, and as the early dew which passeth away.' The *end* is the proof of the matter. When the sun shines, this earth pleases; but let us look towards that eventide and the cool of the day, when the Lord of the vineyard will walk amid the trees of His garden, and say unto His steward, 'Call the labourers, and give them their hire, beginning from the last unto the first.' That evening will be the trial: when the heat, and fever, and noise of the noontide are over, and the light fades, and the prospect saddens, and the shades lengthen, and the busy world is still, and 'the door shall be shut in the streets, and the daughters of music shall be brought low, and fears shall be in the way, and the almond-tree shall flourish, and the grasshopper shall be a burden, and desire shall fail,' and 'the pitcher shall be broken at the fountain, and the wheel broken at the cistern'[2] ...

The Work of the Christian   SD p. 11.   23 January, 1842

1   Jer 13, 16
2   Eccles 12, 4f

The last shall be first and the first last, for many are called, but few are chosen. Such are the words with which the Gospel of this day ends, which is the Parable of the Labourers in the Vineyard. In that parable, you know well, my brethren, the Master of the Vineyard calls into his Vineyard all the labourers he can get together. He calls them in at different times, some in the morning, some at noon, some shortly before the evening. When the evening is come, he bids his paymaster call them together and give them their wages for the day past. It is very plain what this means. The Master of the Vineyard is our Lord and Saviour. We are the labourers. The evening is the hour of death, when we shall each receive the reward of our labour, if we have laboured well.

Preparation for the Judgement   CS p. 32.   20 February, 1848. St Chad's, Birmingham

Twenty-sixth Sunday of the Year

Ezek 18, 25–28; Phil 2, 1–11; Matt 21, 28–32

Doing the Father's Will

Our religious professions are at a far greater distance from our acting upon them, than we ourselves are aware. We know generally that it is our duty to serve God, and we resolve we will do so faithfully. We are sincere in thus generally desiring and purposing to be obedient, and we think we are in earnest; yet we go away, and presently, without any struggle of mind or apparent change of purpose, almost without knowing ourselves what we do, – we go away and do the very contrary to the resolution we have expressed. This inconsistency is exposed by our Blessed Lord in the second part of the parable which I have taken for my text. You will observe, that in the case of the first son, who said he would not go to work, and yet did go, it is said, 'afterward he repented'; he underwent a positive change of purpose. But in the case of the second, it is merely said, 'he answered, I go, Sir; and went not'; – for here there was *no* revolution of sentiment, nothing deliberate; he merely acted according to his habitual frame of mind; he did *not* go to work, because it was contrary to his general character to work; only he did not know this. He said, 'I go, Sir,' sincerely, from the feeling of the moment; but when the words were out of his mouth, then they were forgotten. It was like the wind blowing against a stream, which seems for a moment to change its course in consequence, but in fact flows down as before.

   To this subject I shall now call your attention, as drawn from the latter part of this parable, passing over the case of the repentant son, which would form a distinct subject in itself. 'He answered and said, I go, Sir; and went not.' We promise to serve God: we do not perform; and that not from deliberate faithlessness in the particular case, but because it is our nature, our *way* not to obey, and *we* do not know this; we do not know ourselves, or what we are promising.

Promising without Doing   PPS I p. 165–6.   30 October, 1831

Twenty-seventh Sunday of the Year

Isa 5, 1–7; Phil 4, 6–9; Matt 21, 33–43

He came into his own Vineyard ...

Or take another instance, not so shocking in its circumstances, yet introducing us to another distinction, in which Christ's passion exceeds that of any innocent sufferers, such as I have supposed. When Joseph was sent by his father to his brethren on a message of love, they, when they saw him, said, 'Behold, this dreamer cometh; come now, therefore, and let us slay him.'[1] They did not kill him, however, but they put him in a pit in spite of the anguish of his soul, and sold him as a slave to the Ishmaelites, and he was taken down into a foreign country, where he had no friends. Now this was most cruel and most cowardly in the sons of Jacob; and what is so especially shocking in it is, that Joseph was not only innocent and defenceless, their younger brother whom they ought to have protected, but besides that, he was so confiding and loving, that he need not have come to them, that he would not at all have been in their power, *except* for his desire to do them service. Now, whom does this history remind us of but of Him concerning whom the Master of the vineyard said, on sending Him to the husbandmen, 'They will reverence My Son'? 'But when the husbandmen saw the Son, they said among themselves, This is the Heir, come, let us kill Him, and let us seize on His inheritance. And they caught Him, and cast Him out of the vineyard, and slew Him.' Here, then, is an additional circumstance of cruelty to affect us in Christ's history, such as is suggested in Joseph's, but which no instance of a brute animal's or of a child's sufferings can have; our Lord was not only guiltless and defenceless, but He had come among His persecutors in love.

The Crucifixion   PPS VII p. 139–40.   25 March. 1842

---

1   Gen. 37, 19. 20.

Twenty-eighth Sunday of the Year

Isa 25, 6 – 10; Phil 4, 12 – 14. 19 – 20; Matt 22, 1 – 14

Christ made his feast for all

Do we never hear it said, that the daily Service of the Church is unnecessary? Is it never hinted that it is scarcely worth while to keep it up unless we get numbers to attend it, as if one single soul, if but one, were not precious enough for Christ's love and His Church's rearing? Is it never objected, that a partially-filled Church is a discouraging sight, as if, after all, our Lord Jesus had chosen the many and not the few to be His true disciples? Is it never maintained, that a Christian minister is off his post unless he is for ever labouring for the heartless many, instead of ministering to the more religious few? Alas! there must be something wrong among us; when our defenders recommend the Church on the mere plea of its activity, its popularity, and its visible usefulness, and would scarcely scruple to give us up, had we *not* the many on our side! If our ground of boasting be, that rich men, and mighty men, and many men love us, it never can be a religious boast, and may be our condemnation. Christ made His feast for 'the poor, the maimed, the lame, and the blind.' It is the widow and the fatherless, the infirm, the helpless, the devoted, bound together in prayer, who are the strength of the Church. It is their prayers, be they many or few, the prayers of Mary and such as Mary, who are the safety, under Christ, of those who with Paul and Barnabas fight the Lord's battles. 'It is but lost labour to rise up early, to sit up late, to eat the bread of sorrows,'[1] if prayers are discontinued. It is mere infatuation, if we think to resist the enemies who at this moment are at our doors, if our Churches remain shut, and we give up to prayer but a few minutes in the day.

The Good Part of Mary   PPS III p. 332 – 3.   26 October, 1834

1   Ps 127, 2

Twenty-ninth Sunday of the Year

Isa 45, 1. 4–6; 1 Thess 1. 1–5; Matt 22, 15–21

Church and State

But I have more to say on this subject, perhaps too much, when I go on, as I now do to contemplate the Christian Church, when persecution was exchanged for establishment, and her enemies became her children. As she resisted and defied her persecutors, so she ruled her convert people. And surely this was but natural, and will startle those only to whom the subject is new. If the Church is independent of the State, so far as she is a messenger from God, therefore, should the State, with its high officials and its subject masses, come into her communion, it is plain that they must at once change hostility into submission. There was no middle term; either they must deny her claim to divinity or humble themselves before it, – that is, as far as the domain of religion extends, and that domain is a wide one. They could not place God and man on one level. We see this principle carried out among ourselves in all sects every day, though with greater or less exactness of application, according to the supernatural power which they ascribe to their ministers or clergy.

The Ancient Church   Diff II p. 200–1 (Letter to the Duke of Norfolk) 1874

The Roman Church then has become political;[1] but let us of the present day beware of running into the other extreme, and of supposing that, because Christ's Kingdom is not based upon this world, that it is not connected with it. Surely it was established here for the sake of this world, and must ever act in it, as if a part of it, though its origin is from above. Like the Angels which appeared to the Patriarchs, it is a Heavenly Messenger in human form. In its Polity, its Public Assemblies, its Rules and Ordinances, its Censures, and its Possessions, it is a visible body, and, to appearance, an institution of this world. It is no faulty zeal to labour to preserve it in the form in which Christ gave it.

Christian Zeal   PPS II p. 390–1.   Nov/Dec 1834

---

1   This reflects Newman's criticism of Daniel O'Connell and Irish Catholic MPs in allying themselves with dissenters on questions of ecclesiastical reform.

Thirtieth Sunday of the Year

Exod 22, 20–26; 1 Thess 1, 5–10; Matt 22, 34–40

The Law written in our hearts

Faith is the first element of *religion*, and love, of *holiness*; and as holiness and religion are distinct, yet united, so are love and faith. Holiness can exist without religion; religion cannot exist without holiness. Baptized infants, before they come to years of understanding, are holy; they are not religious. Holiness is love of the Divine Law. When God regenerates an infant, He imparts to it the gift of His Holy Spirit; and what is the Spirit thus imparted but the Law written on its heart? Such was the promise, 'I will put My laws into their mind, and write them in their hearts.' And hence it is said, 'This is the love of God, that we keep His *commandments.'*[1] God comes to us as a Law, before He comes as a Lawgiver; that is, He sets up His throne within us, and enables us to obey Him, before we have learned to reflect on our own sensations, and to know the voice of God.

Faith and Love   PPS IV p. 312.   25 February, 1838

---

1   Heb 8, 10. 1 John 5, 3.

Thirty-first Sunday of the Year

Mal 1, 14−2, 2. 8−10; 1 Thess 2, 7−9. 13; Matt 23, 1−12

The Outward Profession of Faith

We have dropped the show of fasting, which (it so happens) the world at the present day derides. Are we quite sure that if fasting were in honour, we should not begin to hold fasts, as the Pharisees? Thus we seek the praise of men. But in all this, how are we, in any good measure, following *God's* guidance and promises?

We see, then, how seasonable is our Lord's warning to us, His disciples, first of all, to beware of the leaven of the Pharisees, which is hypocrisy: professing without practising. He warns us against it as *leaven*, as a subtle insinuating evil which will silently spread itself throughout the whole character, if we suffer it. He warns us, His disciples, lovingly considerate for us, lest we make ourselves a scorn and derision to the profane multitude, who throng around to gaze curiously, or malevolently, or selfishly, at His doings. *They* seek Him, not as adoring Him for His miracles' sake, but, if so be that they can obtain any thing from Him, or can please their natural tastes while they profess to honour Him; and in time of trial they desert Him. They make a gain of godliness, or a fashion. So He speaks not to *them*, but to us, His little flock, His Church, to whom it has been His Father's good pleasure to give the kingdom;[1] and He bids us take heed of falling, as the Pharisees did before us, and like them coming short of our reward.

Profession without Practice   PPS I p. 134−5.   9 October, 1831

---

[1] Luke 12, 32

Now this age is as removed in distance, as in character, from that of the Greek philosopher; yet who will say that the religion which it acts upon is very different from the religion of the heathen? Of course I understand well, that it might know, and that it will say, a great many things foreign and contrary to heathenism. I am well aware that the theology of this age is very different from what it was two thousand years ago. I know men profess a great deal, and boast that they are Christians, and speak of Christianity as being a religion of the heart; but, when we put aside words and professions, and try to discover what their religion is, we shall find, I fear, that the great mass of men in fact get rid of all religion that is inward; that they lay no stress on acts of faith, hope, and charity, on simplicity of intention, purity of motive, or mortification of the thoughts; that they confine themselves to two or three virtues, superficially practised; that they know not the words contrition, penance, and pardon; and that they think and argue that, after all, if a man does his duty in the world, according to his vocation, he cannot fail to go to heaven, however little he may do besides, nay, however much, in other matters, he may do that is undeniably unlawful.

The Religion of the Pharisee, the Religion of Mankind   OS p. 25–6.   10th after Pentecost, 1856

Thirty-second Sunday of the Year

Wisd 6, 12–16; 1 Thess 4, 13–18; Matt 25, 1–13

Those who watch ...

Let us then consider this most serious question, which concerns every one of us so nearly; – What it is to *watch* for Christ? He says, '*Watch* ye therefore, for ye know not when the Master of the house cometh; at even, or at midnight, or at the cock-crowing, or in the morning; lest coming suddenly He find you sleeping. And what I say unto you, I say unto all, *Watch*.' And again, 'If the goodman of the house had known what hour the thief would come, he would have *watched*, and not have suffered his house to be broken through.' A like warning is given elsewhere both by our Lord and by His Apostles. For instance; we have the parable of the Ten Virgins, five of whom were wise and five foolish; on whom the bridegroom, after tarrying came suddenly, and five were found without oil. On which our Lord says, '*Watch* therefore, for ye know neither the day nor the hour wherein the Son of man cometh.' ...

He watches for Christ who has a sensitive, eager, apprehensive mind; who is awake, alive, quick-sighted, zealous in seeking and honouring Him; who looks out for Him in all that happens, and who would not be surprised, who would not be over-agitated or overwhelmed, if he found that He was coming at once.

And he watches *with* Christ, who, while he looks on to the future, looks back on the past, and does not so contemplate what his Saviour has purchased for him, as to forget what He has suffered for him. He watches with Christ, who ever commemorates and renews in his own person Christ's Cross and Agony, and gladly takes up that mantle of affliction which Christ wore here, and left behind Him when he ascended. ...

This then is to watch; to be detached from what is present, and to live in what is unseen; to live in the thought of Christ as He came once, and as He will come again; to desire His second coming, from our affectionate and grateful remembrance of His first.

Watching   PPS IV p. 320, 323–324, 325.   3 December, 1837

Thirty-third Sunday of the Year

Prov 31, 10–13. 19–20. 30–31; 1 Thess 5, 1–6; Matt 25, 14–30

The Use of our Talents

Another class of involuntary sins are such as arise from want of self-command; that is, from the mind being possessed of more light than strength, the conscience begin informed, but the governing principle weak. The soul of man is intended to be a well-ordered polity, in which there are many powers and faculties, and each has its due place; and for these to exceed their limits is sin; yet they cannot be kept within those limits except by being governed, and we are unequal to this task of governing ourselves except after long habit. While we are learning to govern ourselves, we are constantly exposed to the risk, or rather to the occurrence of numberless failures. We have failures by the way, though we triumph in the end; and thus, as I just now implied, the process of learning to obey God is, in one sense, a process of sinning, from the nature of the case. We have much to be forgiven; nay, we have the more to be forgiven the more we attempt. The higher our aims, the greater our risks. They who venture much with their talents, gain much, and in the end they hear the words, 'Well done, good and faithful servant'; but they have so many losses in trading by the way, that to themselves they seem to do nothing but fail. They cannot believe that they are making any progress; and though they do, yet surely they have much to be forgiven in all their services. They are like David, men of blood; they fight the good fight of faith, but they are polluted with the contest.

Sins of Infirmity   PPS V p. 213–4.   1 April, 1838

Now I say, agreeably with this, we shall find our Saviour's parables divide Christians into two states, those who continue in God's favour, and those who lose it; and those who continue in it are said to be, not those who merely have repentance and faith, who sin, but ever wash out their sins by coming for pardon, but those who do not sin; − not those whose one great aim is to obtain *forgiveness*, but those who (though they abound in infirmities, and so far have much to be forgiven) yet are best *described* by saying that they aim at *increasing* their talents, aim at 'laying up for themselves a good foundation for the time to come, that they may lay hold of eternal life.'[1]

The State of Salvation　PPS V p. 184−5.　18 March, 1838

1　1 Tim 6, 19

Our Lord Jesus Christ, Universal King (34th Sunday)

Ezek 34, 11–12. 15–17; 1 Cor 15, 20–26. 28; Matt 25, 31–46

Those for whom the Kingdom is prepared

In the description our Lord gives us of the Last Judgment, He tells us He shall say to them on His right hand, 'Come, ye blessed of My Father, inherit the kingdom *prepared* for you from the foundation of the world.' Here we have the same expression. Who then are the heirs for whom the Kingdom is prepared? He tells us expressly, those who fed the hungry and thirsty, lodged the stranger, clothed the naked, visited the sick, came to the prisoners, for His sake. Consider again an earlier passage in the same chapter. To whom is it that He will say, 'Enter thou into the joy of thy Lord'? – to those whom He can praise as 'good and faithful servants,' who have been 'faithful over a few things.' These two passages then carry our search just to the very point which is suggested by the text. They lead us *from* the thought of God and Christ, and throw us upon human agency and responsibility, for the solution of the question; and they finally lodge us there, *unless* indeed other texts of Scripture can be produced to lead us on further still. We know for certain that they for whom the Kingdom is prepared are the humble, the charitable, and the diligent in the improvement of their gifts; to which another text (for instance) adds the spiritually-minded: – 'Eye hath not seen the things which God hath *prepared* for them that *love* Him.' Is this as far as we can go? Does it now depend ultimately on ourselves, or on any one else, that we come to be humble, charitable, diligent, and lovers of God?

St. James.   Human Responsibility PPS II p. 321–2.   Jan/Feb 1835

First Sunday of Advent

Isa 63, 16−17. 64, 1. 3−8; 1 Cor 1, 3−9; Mark 13, 33−37

The Lord comes unexpectedly ...

Our Saviour gave this warning when He was leaving this world, − leaving it, that is, as far as His visible presence is concerned. He looked forward to the many hundred years which were to pass before He came again. He knew His own purpose and His Father's purpose gradually to leave the world to itself, gradually to withdraw from it the tokens of His gracious presence. He contemplated, as contemplating all things, the neglect of Him which would spread even among his professed followers; the daring disobedience, and the loud words, which would be ventured against Him and His Father by many whom He had regenerated: and the coldness, cowardice, and tolerance of error which would be displayed by others, who did not go so far as to speak or to act against Him. He foresaw the state of the world and the Church, as we see it this day, when his prolonged absence has made it practically thought, that He never will come back in visible presence: and in the text He mercifully whispers into our ears, not to trust in what we see, not to share in that general unbelief, not to be carried away by the world, but to 'take heed, watch, pray,' and look out for His coming.

Watching   PPS IV p. 319−20.   3 December, 1837

Second Sunday of Advent

Isa 40, 1–5. 9–11; 2 Pet 3, 8–14; Mark 1, 1–8

True Detachment, a Preparation for Christ

Our Saviour says, 'Narrow is the way.' This, of course, must not be interpreted without great caution; yet surely the whole tenor of the Inspired Volume leads us to believe that His Truth will not be heartily received by the many, that it is against the current of human feeling and opinion, and the course of the world, and so far forth as it *is* received by a man, will be opposed by himself, *i.e.* by his old nature which remains about him, next by all others, so far forth as they have not received it. 'The light shining in darkness' is the token of true religion; and, though doubtless there are seasons when a sudden enthusiasm arises in favour of the Truth (as in the history of St. John the Baptist, in whose 'light' the Jews 'were willing for a season to rejoice,'[1]) so as even 'to be baptized of him, confessing their sins'[2]), yet such a popularity of the Truth is *but* sudden, comes at once and goes at once, has no regular growth, no abiding stay. It is error alone which grows and is received heartily on a large scale. St. Paul has set up his warning against our supposing Truth will ever be heartily accepted, whatever show there may be of a general profession of it, in his last Epistle, where he tells Timothy, among other sad prophecies, that 'evil men and seducers shall wax worse and worse.'[3] Truth, indeed, has that power in it, that it forces men to profess it in words; but when they go on to act, instead of obeying *it*, they substitute some idol in the place of it.

Self-denial the Test of Religious Earnestness   PPS I p. 61–2.   22 December, 1833

---

1   John 5, 35
2   Matt 3, 6
3   2 Tim 3, 13

We must not only have faith in Him, but must wait on Him; not only must hope, but must watch for Him; not only love Him, but must long for Him; not only obey Him, but must look out, look up earnestly for our reward, which is Himself. We must not only make Him the Object of our faith, hope, and charity, but we must make it our duty not to believe the world, not to hope in the world, not to love the world. We must resolve not to hang on the world's opinion, or study its wishes. It is our mere wisdom to be thus detached from all things below.

Waiting for Christ   OS p. 34.   27th after Pentecost, 1856

Third Sunday of Advent

Isa 61, 1–2. 10–11; 1 Thess 5, 16–24; John 1, 6–8. 19–28

'He will baptize you with the Holy Spirit'

Such is St. Paul's doctrine after Christ had died; St. John the Baptist teaches the same beforehand. 'I indeed baptize you with water unto repentance but he shall baptize you with the Holy Ghost and with fire.' Doubtless there is an allusion here to the special descent of the Spirit at Pentecost; but, even taking it as such, the fulfilment of the Baptist's words then, becomes a pledge to us of the fulfilment of our Saviour's words to Nicodemus to the end of time. He who came by fire at Pentecost, will, as He has said, come by water now. But we may reasonably consider these very words of the Baptist as referring to ordinary Christian Baptism, as well as to the miraculous Baptism of the Apostles. As if he said, 'Christ's Baptism shall not be mere water, as mine is. What you see of it indeed is water, but that is but the subordinate element of it; for it is water endued with high and supernatural qualities. Would it not surprise you if water burned like fire? Such, and more than such, is the mystery of that water which He shall pour out on you, having a searching and efficacious influence upon the soul itself.'

Regenerating Baptism   PPS III p. 280.   Nov/Dec 1834

Fourth Sunday of Advent

2 Sam 7, 1–5. 8–12. 14. 16; Rom 16, 25–27; Luke 1, 26–38

The Word of Life born of the Holy Mother of God

Immortal nature is implied. 'That *Holy* Thing' which was born of Mary, was 'the Son,' not of man, but 'of God.' Others have all been born in sin, 'after Adam's own likeness, in His image,'[1] and, being born in sin, they are heirs to corruption. 'By one man sin entered into the world, and death,' and all its consequences, 'by sin.' Not one human being comes into existence without God's discerning evidences of sin attendant on his birth. But when the Word of Life was manifested in our flesh, the Holy Ghost displayed that creative hand by which, in the beginning, Eve was formed.

Easter Day. Christ, a Quickening Spirit　PPS II p. 140.　3 April, 1831

Christmastide – as for Year A

1　Gen 5, 3

Sunday in the Octave of Christmas: The Holy Family

Gen 15, 1–6. 21, 1–3; Heb 11, 8. 11–12. 17–18; Luke 2, 22–40

A Little Child is brought to The Temple

This, then, is the event in our Saviour's infancy which we this day celebrate; His Presentation in the Temple when His Virgin Mother was ceremonially purified. It was made memorable at the time by the hymns and praises of Simeon and Anna, to whom He was then revealed. And there were others, besides these, who had been 'looking for redemption in Jerusalem,' who were also vouchsafed a sight of the Infant Saviour. But the chief importance of this event consists in its being a fulfilment of prophecy. Malachi had announced the Lord's visitation of His Temple in these words, 'The Lord whom ye seek shall suddenly come to His Temple';[1] words which, though variously fulfilled during His ministry, had their first accomplishment in the humble ceremony commemorated on this day. And, when we consider the grandeur of the prediction, and how unostentatious this accomplishment was, we are led to muse upon God's ways, and to draw useful lessons for ourselves. This is the reflection which I propose to make upon the subject of this Festival.

I say, we are to-day reminded of the noiseless course of God's providence, – His tranquil accomplishment, in the course of nature, of great events long designed; and again, of the suddenness and stillness of His visitations. Consider what the occurrence in question consists in. A little child is brought to the Temple, as all first-born children were brought. There is nothing here uncommon or striking, so far. His parents are with him, poor people, bringing the offering of pigeons or doves, for the purification of the mother. They are met in the Temple by an old man, who takes the child in his arms, offers a thanksgiving to God, and blesses the parents; and next are joined by a woman of great age, a widow of eighty-four years, who had exceeded the time of useful service, and seemed to be but a fit prey for death. She gives thanks

also, and speaks concerning the child to other persons who are present.
Then all retire.

Purification of the Blessed Virgin. Secrecy of Divine Visitations PPS II p. 108–9
2 February, 1831

January 1st, Epiphany and 2nd Sunday after Christmas — as for Year A

1   Mal 3, 1

The Baptism of the Lord (First Sunday after Epiphany)

Isa 55, 1–11; 1 John 5, 1–9; Mark 1, 7–11

He came to be baptised . . .

When our Lord came to John to be baptized, He gave this reason for it, 'Thus it becometh us to fulfil all righteousness'; which seems to mean, – 'It is becoming in Me, the expected Christ, to conform in all respects to all the rites and ceremonies of Judaism, to everything hitherto accounted sacred and binding.' Hence it was that he came to be baptized, to show that it was not His intention in any way to dishonour the Established Religion, but to fulfil it even in those parts of it (such as Baptism) which were later than the time of Moses; and especially to acknowledge thereby the mission of John the Baptist, His forerunner. And those ordinances which Moses himself was commissioned to appoint, had still greater claim to be respected and observed. It was on this account that He was circumcised, as we this day commemorate; in order, that is, to show that He did not renounce the religion of Abraham, to whom God gave circumcision, or of Moses, by whom it was embodied in the Jewish Law.

The Circumcision of Christ. Ceremonies of the Church   PPS II p. 69–70
1 January, 1831

First Sunday of Lent

Gen 9, 8–15; 1 Pet 3, 18–22; Mark 1, 12–15

A Second Adam to the fight and to the rescue came

Again, there is something of mystery in the connection of His temptation with the descent of the Holy Ghost upon Him on His baptism. After the voice from heaven had proclaimed, 'This is My beloved Son, in whom I am well pleased,' *'immediately,'* as St. Mark says, 'the Spirit *driveth* Him into the wilderness.' As if there were some connection, beyond our understanding, between His baptism and temptation, the first act of the Holy Spirit is forthwith to 'drive Him' (whatever is meant by the word) into the wilderness. Observe, too, that it was almost from this solemn recognition, 'This is My beloved Son,' that the Devil took up the temptation, *'If* Thou be the Son of God command that these stones be made bread';[1] yet what his thoughts and designs were we cannot even conjecture. All we see is a renewal, apparently, of Adam's temptation, in the person of the 'second Man.'

The Humiliation of the Eternal Son   PPS III p. 158–9.   8 March, 1835

---

1   Matt 4, 3.

Second Sunday of Lent

Gen 22, 1–2. 9–13. 15–18; Rom 8, 31–34; Mark 9, 2–10

He was transfigured . . .

In that day we shall enter, if we be worthy, the fullness of that glory, of which the three Apostles had the foretaste in the moment of Transfiguration. All is darkness here, all is bright in heaven. All is disorder here, all is order there. All is noise here and there there is stillness, or if sounds are heard, they are the sweet sounds of the eternal harps on which the praises of God are sung. Here we are in a state of uncertainty; we do not know what is to happen. The Church suffers; her goodly portion and her choice inheritance suffer; the vineyard is laid waste; there is persecution and war; and Satan rages and afflicts when he cannot destroy. But all this will be set right in the world to come, and if St. Peter could say at the Transfiguration, 'It is good to be here', much more shall we have cause to say so when we see the face of God. For then we shall be like our Lord Himself, we shall have glorified bodies, as He had then and has now. We shall have put off flesh and blood, and receive our bodies at the last day, the same indeed, but incorruptible, spiritual bodies, which will be able to see and enjoy the presence of God in a way which was beyond the three Apostles in the days of their mortality.

The World and Sin   CS p. 90–1. 2nd Lent.   19 March, 1848, St Chad's Birmingham

It was, in one sense, a miracle; yet it had no beneficent purpose or lasting consequence, as is usual with our Lord's miracles, and it took place in private. But, surely, it is of a doctrinal nature, being nothing less than a figurative exhibition of the blessed truth contained in the texts under review, a vision of the glorious Kingdom which He set up on the earth on His coming. He said to His Apostles, 'I tell you of a truth, there be some standing here which shall not taste of death till they *see the Kingdom of God.*' Then, 'after six days Jesus taketh Peter, James, and John his brother, and bringeth them up into a high mountain apart, and was transfigured before them. And as He prayed the fashion of His countenance was altered, and His raiment was white and glistening. And His face did shine as the sun, and His raiment was white as the light. ... And behold there talked with Him two men, which were Moses and Elias, who appeared in glory. ... But Peter and they that were with him were heavy with sleep; and when they were awake, *they saw His glory.*' Such is the Kingdom of God; Christ the centre of it, His glory the light of it, the Just made perfect His companions, and the Apostles His witnesses to their brethren. It realizes what the ancient Saints saw by glimpses – Jacob at Bethel, Moses on Sinai.

The Gift of the Spirit   PPS III p. 265–6.   8 November, 1835

Cf. Feast of the Transfiguration

Third Sunday of Lent

Exod 20, 1–17; 1 Cor 1, 22–25; John 2, 13–25

The Zeal of Christ

I do not deny that this view of the subject is different from that which certain principles and theories now current in the world would lead us to adopt; but this surely is no reason that it should not be true, unless indeed, amid the alternate successes of good and evil, there be any infallible token given us to ascertain the superior illumination of the present century over all those which have preceded it. In fact we have no standard of Truth at all but the Bible, and to that I would appeal. 'To the Law and to the Testimony'; if the opinions of the day are conformable to it, let them remain in honour, but if not, however popular they may be at the moment, they will surely come to nought. It is the present fashion to call Zeal by the name of intolerance, and to account intolerance the chief of sins; that is, any earnestness for one opinion above another concerning God's nature, will, and dealings with man, – or, in other words, any earnestness for the Faith once delivered to the Saints, any earnestness for Revelation as such. Surely, in this sense, the Apostles were the most intolerant of men.

St. Simon and St. Jude. Christian Zeal   PPS II p. 384.   Nov/Dec 1834

Fourth Sunday of Lent

2 Chr 33, 14−16. 19−23; Eph 2, 4−10; John 3, 14−21

'The Son of Man must be lifted up'

It must not be supposed, because the doctrine of the Cross makes us sad, that therefore the Gospel is a sad religion.

It only forbids us to *begin* with enjoyment. It only says, If you begin with pleasure, you will end with pain. It bids us begin with the Cross of Christ, and in that Cross we shall at first find sorrow, but in a while peace and comfort will rise out of that sorrow. Let us begin with faith; let us begin with Christ; let us begin with His Cross and the humiliation to which it leads. Let us first be drawn to Him who is lifted up, that so He may, with Himself, freely give us all things. Let us 'seek first the Kingdom of God and His righteousness,' and then all those things of this world 'will be added to us.' They alone are able truly to enjoy this world, who begin with the world unseen. They alone enjoy it, who have first abstained from it. They alone can truly feast, who have first fasted; they alone are able to use the world, who have learned not to abuse it; they alone inherit it, who take it as a shadow of the world to come, and who for that world to come relinquish it.

The Cross of Christ the Measure of the World   PPS VI p. 90, 91, 93.   9 April, 1841

Fifth Sunday of Lent

Jer 31, 31–34; Heb 5, 7–9; John 12, 20–33

Gaze upon the Cross

The world, at first sight, appears *made* for pleasure, and the vision of Christ's Cross is a solemn and sorrowful sight interfering with this appearance. Be it so; but why may it not be our duty to abstain from enjoyment notwithstanding, if it was a duty even in Eden?

But again; it is but a superficial view of things to say that this life is made for pleasure and happiness. To those who look under the surface, it tells a very different tale. The doctrine of the Cross does but teach, though infinitely more forcibly, still after all it does but teach the very same lesson which this world teaches to those who live long in it, who have much experience in it, who know it. The world is sweet to the lips, but bitter to taste. It pleases at first, but not at last. It looks gay on the outside, but evil and misery lie concealed within. When a man has passed a certain number of years in it, he cries out with the Preacher, 'Vanity of vanities, all is vanity.' Nay, if he has not religion for his guide, he will be forced to go further, and say, 'All is vanity and vexation of spirit'; all is disappointment; all is sorrow; all is pain. The sore judgments of God upon sin are concealed within it, and force a man to grieve whether he will or no. Therefore the doctrine of the Cross of Christ does but anticipate for us our experience of the world. It is true, it bids us.

Again: look at misery, look at poverty and destitution, look at oppression and captivity; go where food is scanty, and lodging unhealthy. Consider pain and suffering, diseases long or violent, all that is frightful and revolting. Would you know how to rate all these? gaze upon the Cross.

Thus in the Cross, and Him who hung upon it, all things meet; all things subserve it, all things need it. It is their centre and their interpretation. For He was lifted up upon it, that He might draw all men and all things unto Him.

But it will be said, that the view which the Cross of Christ imparts to us of human life and of the world, is not that which we should take, if left to ourselves; that it is not an obvious view; that if we look at things on their surface, they are far more bright and sunny than they appear when viewed in the light which this season casts upon them. The world seems made for the enjoyment of just such a being as man, and man is put into it. He has the *capacity* of enjoyment, and the world supplies the *means*. How natural this, what a simple as well as pleasant philosophy, yet how different from that of the Cross! The doctrine of the Cross, it may be said, disarranges two parts of a system which seem made for each other; it severs the fruit from the eater, the enjoyment from the enjoyer. How does this solve a problem? does it not rather itself create one? ...

The Cross of Christ the Measure of the World   PPS VI p. 86–87.   9 April, 1841

Passion Sunday (Palm Sunday)

Isa 50, 4–7; Phil 2, 6–11; Mark 14, 1–15. 47

And they led Him out to crucify Him

He who thus humbled Himself – being first made man, then dying, and that upon the shameful and agonizing Cross – was the same who from eternity had been 'in the form of God,' and was 'equal with God,' as the Apostle declares in a preceding verse.[1] 'In the beginning was the Word, and the Word was with God; and the Word was God; the same was in the beginning with God'; thus speaks St. John, a second witness to the same great awful truth. And he, too, goes on to say, 'And the Word was made flesh, and dwelt among us.'[2] And at the close of his Gospel, as we know, he gives an account of our Lord's death upon the Cross.

The Incarnate Son, a Sufferer and Sacrifice   PPS VI p. 69.   1 April, 1836

1   Phil 2, 6
2   John 1, 1. 14

The Mass of Easter Night

Rom 6, 3–11; Mark 16, 1–8

Christ is risen indeed!

Such then is our risen Saviour in Himself and towards us: − conceived by the Holy Ghost; holy from the womb; dying, but abhorring corruption; rising again the third day by His own inherent life; exalted as the Son of God and Son of man, to raise us after Him; and filling us incomprehensibly with His immortal nature, till we become like Him; filling us with a spiritual life which may expel the poison of the tree of knowledge, and restore us to God. How wonderful a work of grace! Strange it was that Adam should be our death, but stranger still and very gracious, that God Himself should be our life, by means of that human tabernacle which He has taken on Himself.

O blessed day of the Resurrection, which of old time was called the Queen of Festivals, and raised among Christians an anxious, nay contentious diligence duly to honour it! Blessed day, once only passed in sorrow, when the Lord actually rose, and the disciples believed not; but ever since a day of joy to the faith and love of the Church! In ancient times, Christians all over the world began it with a morning salutation. Each man said to his neighbour, 'Christ is risen'; and his neighbour answered him, 'Christ is risen indeed, and hath appeared unto Simon.' Even to Simon, the coward disciple who denied Him thrice, Christ is risen; even to us, who long ago vowed to obey Him, and have yet so often denied Him before men, so often taken part with sin, and followed the world, when Christ called us another way. 'Christ is risen indeed, and hath appeared to Simon!' to Simon Peter the favoured Apostle, on whom the Church is built, Christ has appeared. He has appeared to His Holy Church first of all, and in the Church He dispenses blessings, such as the world knows not of. Blessed are they if they knew their blessedness, who are allowed, as we are, week after week, and Festival after Festival, to seek and find in that Holy Church the Saviour of their souls!

Easter Day. Christ, a Quickening Spirit   PPS II p. 147–8.   3 April, 1831

Easter Sunday Masses − as for Year A

Second Sunday of Easter

Acts 4, 32–35; 1 John 5, 1–6; John 20, 19–31

Love of God, Love of the Brethren

But what I would to-day draw attention to, is the thought with which I began, viz. the comfort vouchsafed to us in being able to contemplate Him whom the Apostle calls 'the man Christ Jesus,' the Son of God in our flesh. I mean, the thought of Him, 'the beginning of the creation of God,' 'the firstborn of every creature,'[1] binds us together by a sympathy with one another, as much greater than that of mere nature, as Christ is greater than Adam. We were brethren, as being of one nature with him, who was 'of the earth, earthy'; we are now brethren, as being of one nature with 'the Lord from heaven.' All those common feelings, which we have by birth, are far more intimately common to us, now that we have obtained the second birth. Our hopes and fears, likes and dislikes, pleasures and pains, have been moulded upon one model, have been wrought into one image, blended and combined unto 'the measure of the stature of the fulness of Christ.' What they become, who have partaken of 'the Living Bread, which came down from heaven,' the first converts showed, of whom it is said that they 'had all things common'; that 'the multitude of them that believed were of one heart and of one soul'; as having 'one body, and one Spirit, one hope, one Lord, one Faith, one Baptism, one God and Father of all.'[2] Yes, and one thing needful; one narrow way; one business on earth; one and the same enemy; the same dangers; the same temptations; the same afflictions; the same course of life; the same death; the same resurrection; the same judgment.

Christian Sympathy   PPS V p. 119.   17 February, 1839

1   Rev 3, 14; Col 1, 15
2   Acts 2, 44. 4, 32; Eph 4, 4–6

Third Sunday of Easter

Acts 3, 13−15. 17−19; 1 John 2, 1−5; Luke 24, 35−48

So man has seen the Invisible God

The same mixture of fear with comfort is found in the Disciples after His Resurrection. The women departed from the sepulchre 'with fear and great joy.' They 'trembled and were amazed: neither said they any thing to any man, for they were afraid.' The Apostles 'were terrified and affrighted, and supposed that they had seen a spirit.' 'They believed not for joy, and wondered.' And our Lord said to them, 'Why are ye troubled? and why do thoughts arise in your hearts?' On another occasion, 'None of the disciples durst ask him, Who art thou? knowing that it was the Lord' It might be from slowness to believe, or from misconception, or from the mere perplexity of amazement, but so it was; they exulted and they were awed.

Shrinking from Christ's Coming　PPS V p. 46−7.　4 December, 1836

It is plain what is the object of spiritual sight which is vouchsafed us in the Gospel, − 'God manifest in the Flesh.' He who was before unseen has shown Himself in Christ; not merely displayed His glory, as (for instance) in what is called a providence, or visitation, or in miracles, or in the actions and character of inspired men, but really He Himself has come upon earth, and has been seen of men in human form. In the same kind of sense, in which we should say we saw a servant of His, Apostle or Prophet, though we could not see his soul, so man has seen the Invisible God; and we have the history of His sojourn among His creatures in the Gospels.

Easter Monday. Saving Knowledge　PPS II p. 153.　Jan/Feb 1835

Fourth Sunday of Easter

Acts 4, 8–12; 1 John 3, 1–2; John 10, 11–18

The Good Shepherd

So was it all over the world when Christ came in His infinite mercy 'to gather in one the children of God that were scattered abroad.' And though for a moment, when in the conflict with the enemy the good Shepherd had to lay down His life for the sheep, they were left without a guide (according to the prophecy already quoted, 'Smite the Shepherd and the sheep shall be scattered'), yet He soon rose from death to live for ever, according to that other prophecy which said, 'He that scattered Israel will gather him, as a shepherd doth his flock.'[1] And as He says Himself in the parable before us, 'He calleth His own sheep by name and leadeth them out, and goeth before them, and the sheep follow Him, for they know His voice,' so, on His resurrection, while Mary wept, He did call her by her name,[2] and she turned herself and knew Him by the ear whom she had not known by the eye. So, too, He said, 'Simon, son of Jonas, lovest thou Me?'[3] And He added, 'Follow Me.' And so again He and His Angel told the women, 'Behold He goeth before you into Galilee ... go tell My brethren, that they go into Galilee, and there shall they see Me.'

From that time the good Shepherd who took the place of the sheep, and died that they might live for ever, has gone before them: and 'they follow the Lamb whithersoever He goeth';[4] going their way forth by the footsteps of the flock, and feeding their kids beside the shepherds' tents.[5]

The Shepherd of our Souls   PPS VIII p. 232–3.   30 April, 1843

1   Jer. 31, 10
2   John 20, 16
3   John 21, 15
4   Rev. 14, 4
5   S of S. 1, 8

Fifth Sunday of Easter

Acts 9, 26–31; 1 John 3, 18–24; John 15, 1–8

Abiding in Christ

And a third witness that the Christian Election is, like the Jewish, conditional, is our Lord's own declaration, which he left behind Him with His Apostles when He was leaving the world, as recorded by the same Evangelist. 'If a man *abide not in Me,*' He said, 'he is cast forth as a branch, and is withered; and men gather them and cast them into the fire, and they are burned.' And, lest restless and reluctant minds should shelter their opposition to this solemn declaration under some supposed obscurity in the expression of 'abiding in Him,' and say that none abide in Him but the pre-destined, He adds, for the removal of all doubt, '*If ye keep my commandments*, ye shall abide in my love.'

St. Matthias. Divine Decrees PPS II p. 123–4.   24 February, 1832

Sixth Sunday of Easter

Acts 10, 25–26. 34–35. 44–48; 1 John 4, 7–10; John 15, 9–17

Remaining in God's Love

When we say that Christ loves His Church, we mean that He loves, nothing of earthly nature, but the fruit of His own grace; − the varied fruits of His grace in innumerable hearts, viewed as brought together in unity of faith and love and obedience, of sacraments, and doctrine, and order, and worship. The object which He contemplates, which He loves in the Church, is not human nature simply, but human nature illuminated and renovated by His own supernatural power.

Secret Power of Divine Grace   OS p. 57.   28th after Pentecost, 1856

For instance, St. James says, 'The effectual fervent prayer of a *righteous* man availeth much.' St. John, 'Whatsoever we ask, we receive of Him, *because we keep* His commandments, and do those things that are pleasing in His sight.'[1] Next let us weigh carefully our Lord's solemn announcements uttered shortly before His crucifixion, and, though addressed primarily to His Apostles, yet, surely, in their degree belonging to all who 'believe on Him through their word.'

Intercession   PPS III p. 355.   22 February, 1835

1   Jas 5, 16; 1 John 3, 22

'We have no love for Him who alone lasts. We love those things which do not last, but come to an end. Things being thus, he whom we ought to love has determined to win us back to Him. With this object He has come into His own world, in the form of one of us men. And in that human form He opens His arms and woos us to return to Him, our Maker.'

Caecilius in *Callista. A Sketch of the Third Century*   *Call* p. 221 (1855)

The Ascension of the Lord

Acts 1, 1–11; Eph 1, 17–23; Mark 16, 15–20

Sent out by Christ

Christ, we are told, has gone up on high 'to present Himself before the face of God for us.' He has 'entered by His own blood once for all into the Holy Place, having effected eternal redemption.' 'He ever liveth to make intercession for those who come unto God by Him; He has a priesthood which will not pass from Him.' 'We have such an High Priest, who is set on the right hand of the throne of the Majesty in the heavens; a Minister of the Sanctuary, and of the true Tabernacle, which the Lord pitched, and not man.'[1]

PPS II p. 210.   Nov/Dec 1834

1   Heb 9, 12. 24. 25; 7, 24. 25; 8, 1. 2

Let us try to accustom ourselves to this view of the subject. The whole Church, all elect souls, each in its turn, is called to this necessary work. Once it was the turn of others, and now it is our turn. . . . Such is our state; – Angels are looking on, – Christ has gone before, – Christ has given us an example, that we may follow His steps. He went through far more, infinitely more, than we can be called to suffer. Our brethren have gone through much more; and they seem to encourage us by their success, and to sympathize in our essay. Now it is our turn; and all ministering spirits keep silence and look on. O let not your foot slip, or your eye be false, or your ear dull, or your attention flagging! Be not dispirited; be not afraid; keep a good heart; be bold; draw not back; – you will be carried through. Whatever troubles come on you, of mind, body, or estate; from within or from without; from chance or from intent; from friends or foes; – whatever your trouble be, though you be lonely, O children of a heavenly Father, be not afraid! quit you like men in your day; and when it is over, Christ will receive you to Himself, and your heart shall rejoice, and your joy no man taketh from you.

Warfare the condition of Victory   PPS VI p. 230–1.   24 May, 1838

Seventh Sunday of Easter

Acts 1, 15–17. 20–26; 1 John 4, 11–16; John 17, 11–19

'I passed your Word on to them and the World hated them'

For Christ surely had taught them what it was to have their treasure in heaven; and they rejoiced, not that their Lord was gone, but that their hearts had gone with Him. Their hearts were no longer on earth, they were risen aloft. When He died on the Cross, they knew not whither He was gone. Before He was seized, they had said to Him, 'Lord, whither goest Thou? Lord, we know not whither Thou goest?' They could but follow Him to the grave and there mourn, for they knew no better; but now they saw Him ascend on high, and in spirit they ascended with Him. Mary wept at the grave because she thought enemies had taken Him away, and she knew not where they had laid Him. 'Where your treasure is, there will your heart be also.'[1] Mary had no heart left to her, for her treasure was lost; but the Apostles were continually in the Temple, praising and blessing God, for their hearts were in heaven, or, in St. Paul's words, they 'were dead, and their life was hid with Christ in God.'

Strengthened, then, with this knowledge, they were able to face those trials which Christ had first undergone Himself, and had foretold as their portion. 'Whither I go,' He had said to St. Peter, 'thou canst not follow Me now, but thou shalt follow Me afterwards.' And He told them, 'They shall put you out of the synagogues, yea, the time cometh, that whosoever killeth you will think that he doeth God service.'[2] That time was now coming, and they were able to rejoice in what so troubled them forty days before. For they understood the promise, 'To him that overcometh, will I grant to sit with Me in My throne, even as I also overcame, and am set down with My Father in His Throne.'[3]

Warfare the condition of Victory PPS VI p. 226–7. 24 May, 1838

1 Matt 6, 21
2 John 16, 2
3 Rev 3, 21

Pentecost Sunday

Acts 2, 11–11; Gal 5, 16–25; John 15, 26–27. 16, 12–15

If you love me, you will keep my Commandments

The indwelling of the Holy Ghost raises the soul, not only to the thought of God, but of Christ also. St. John says, 'Truly our fellowship is with the Father, and with His Son Jesus Christ.'[1] And our Lord Himself, 'If a man love Me, he will keep My words; and My Father will love him, and We will come unto him, and make our abode with him.' Now, not to speak of other and higher ways in which these texts are fulfilled, one surely consists in that exercise of faith and love in the thought of the Father and Son, which the Gospel, and the Spirit revealing it, furnish to the Christian. The Spirit came especially to 'glorify' Christ; and vouchsafes to be a shining light within the Church and the individual Christian, reflecting the Saviour of the world in all His perfections, all His offices, all His works. He came for the purpose of unfolding what was yet hidden, whilst Christ was on earth; and speaks on the house-tops what was delivered in closets, disclosing Him in the glories of His transfiguration, who once had no comeliness in His outward form, and was but a man of sorrows and acquainted with grief. First, He inspired the Holy Evangelists to record the life of Christ, and directed them which of His words and works to select, which to omit; next, He commented (as it were) upon these, and unfolded their meaning in the Apostolic Epistles. The birth, the life, the death and resurrection of Christ, has been the text which He has illuminated. He has made history to be doctrine; telling us plainly, whether by St. John or St. Paul, that Christ's conception and birth was the real Incarnation of the Eternal Word, – His life, 'God manifest in the Flesh.'

Whitsunday. The Indwelling Spirit   PPS II p. 226–7.   Nov/Dec 1834

---

1   1 John 1, 3

The Most Holy Trinity

Deut 4, 32–34. 39–40; Rom 8, 14–17; Matt 28, 16–20

'Go, make disciples of all the nations'

That in some real sense the Father, and the Son, and the Holy Ghost are They whom we are bound to serve and worship, from whom comes the Gospel of grace, and in whom the profession of Christianity centres, surely is shown, most satisfactorily and indisputably, by the words of this text. When Christ was departing, He gave commission to His Apostles, and taught them what to teach and preach; and first of all they were to introduce their converts into His profession, or into His Church, and that by a solemn rite, which, as He had told Nicodemus at an earlier time, was to convey a high spiritual grace. This solemn and supernatural ordinance of discipleship was to be administered in the Name – of whom? in the Name (can we doubt it?) of Him whose disciples the converts forthwith became; of that God whom, from that day forward, they confessed and adored.

The Mystery of the Holy Trinity   PPS VI p. 343   Date unknown

The Body and Blood of Christ

Exod 24, 3–8; Heb 9, 11–15; Mark 14, 12–16. 22–26

Christ our Sacrifice

There is something very observable and very touching in the earnestness displayed in these words of our Lord, and in the acts which preceded them. He had showed beforehand that great desire, of which He here speaks. That He had thought much of His last passover which He was to eat with His disciples, is plain from the solemnity with which He marked out the place to them, and the display of supernatural knowledge with which He accompanied His directions. 'He sendeth forth two of His disciples,' 'Peter and John,' 'and saith unto them, Go ye into the city, and there shall meet you a man bearing a pitcher of water: follow him. And wheresoever he shall go in, say ye to the good-man of the house,' 'The Master saith, My time is at hand'; I will keep the passover at thy house with My disciples.' And as at His first feast, He had seemed to turn from His Mother's prayer, while He granted it, because of the time, so to His Apostles He foretold, at His second feast, what the power of their prayers should be hereafter, by way of cheering them on His departure. 'Ye now therefore have sorrow, but I will see you again, and your heart shall rejoice, and your joy no man taketh from you. In that day ye shall ask Me nothing. Verily, verily, I say unto you, Whatsoever ye shall ask the Father in My Name, He will give it you.' And again, 'Ye are My friends, if ye do whatsoever I command you. Henceforth I call you not servants, for the servant knoweth not what his lord doeth; but I have called you friends, for all things that I have heard of My Father, I have made known unto you.' In the gifts then promised to the Apostles after the Resurrection, we may learn the present influence and power of the Mother of God.

Such seems to be the connexion between the feast with which our Lord began, and that with which He ended His ministry. Nay, may we not add without violence, that in the former feast He had in mind and intended to foreshadow the latter? for what was that first miracle by which He manifested His glory in the former, but the strange and awful change of the element of water into wine? and what did He in the latter, but change the Paschal Supper and the typical lamb into the sacrament of His atoning sacrifice, and the creatures of bread and wine into the verities of His most precious Body and Blood. He began His ministry with a miracle; He ended it with a greater.

Our Lord's Last Supper and His First   SD p. 26. 37–8.   16 October 1842 and 26 February, 1843

> And that a higher gift than grace
> Should flesh and blood refine,
> God's Presence and His very Self,
> And Essence all-divine.

Dream of Gerontius   VV p. 360.   (January, 1865)

The Sacred Heart of Jesus

Hos 11, 1.3−4. 8−9; Eph 3, 8−12. 14−19; John 19, 31−37

'They will look on Him whom they have pierced'

Yes, we shall all of us, for weal or for woe, one day see that holy Countenance which wicked men struck and dishonoured; we shall see those Hands that were nailed to the cross; that Side which was pierced. We shall see all this; and it will be the sight of the Living God. ...

Almost all religions have their outward cleansings; they feel the need of man, though they cannot supply it. Even the Jewish system, though Divine, effected nothing here; its washings were but carnal; the blood of bulls and goats was but earthy and unprofitable. Even St. John's baptism, our Lord's forerunner, had no inward propitiatory power. Christ was not yet crucified. But when that long-expected season came, when the Son of God had solemnly set Himself apart as a Victim in the presence of His twelve Apostles, and had gone into the garden, and before three of them had undergone His agony and bloody sweat, and then had been betrayed, buffeted, spit upon, scourged, and nailed to the cross, till He died, then He with His last breath said, 'It is finished'; and from that time the virtue of the Highest went forth through His wounds and with His blood, for the pardon and regeneration of man; and hence it is that baptism has its power.

The Incarnate Son, a Sufferer and Sacrifice   PPS VI p. 76, 77−8.   1 April, 1836

This being the case, the great and awful doctrine of the Cross of Christ, which we now commemorate, may fitly be called, in the language of figure, the *heart* of religion. The heart may be considered as the seat of life; it is the principle of motion, heat, and activity; from it the blood goes to and fro to the extreme parts of the body. It sustains the man in his powers and faculties; it enables the brain to think; and when it is touched, man dies. And in like manner the sacred doctrine of Christ's Atoning Sacrifice is the vital principle on which the Christian lives, and without which Christianity is not.

The Cross of Christ the Measure of the World   PPS VI p. 89.   9 April, 1841

Second Sunday of the Year

1 Sam 3, 3–10. 19; 1 Cor 6, 13–15. 17–20; John 1, 35–42

'We have found the Messiah'

St. Andrew, who was already one of St. John's disciples, was attending on his master with another, when, as it happened, Jesus passed by. The Baptist, who had from the first declared his own subordinate place in the dispensation which was then opening, took this occasion of pointing out to his two disciples Him in whom it centred. He said, 'Behold the Lamb of God'; this is He of whom I spake, whom the Father has chosen and sent, the true sacrificial Lamb, by whose sufferings the sins of the world will be expiated. On hearing this, the two disciples (Andrew, I say, being one of them) straightway left John and followed Christ. He turned round and asked them, 'What seek ye?' They expressed their desire to be allowed to wait upon His teaching; and He suffered them to accompany Him home, and to pass that day with Him. What he said to them is not told us; but St. Andrew received such confirmation of the truth of the Baptist's words, that in consequence he went after his own brother to tell him what he had found. 'He first findeth his own brother Simon, and saith unto him, We have found the Messias ... and he brought him to Jesus.'

St. Andrew. The World's Benefactors PPS II p. 1–2. 30 November, 1830

Third Sunday of the Year

Jonah 3, 1–5. 10; 1 Cor 7, 29–31; Mark 1, 14–20

'. . . For they were Fishermen'

St. Paul says that 'not many wise men according to the flesh, not many mighty, not many noble,'[1] became Christians. He, indeed, is one of those few; so were others his contemporaries, and, as time went on, the number of these exceptions increased, so that converts were found, not a few, in the high places of the Empire, and in the schools of philosophy and learning; but still the rule held, that the great mass of Christians were to be found in those classes which were of no account in the world, whether on the score of rank or of education.

We all know this was the case with our Lord and His Apostles. It seems almost irreverent to speak of their temporal employments, when we are so simply accustomed to consider them in their spiritual associations; but it is profitable to remind ourselves that our Lord Himself was a sort of smith, and made ploughs and cattle-yokes. Four Apostles were fishermen, one a petty tax collector, two husbandmen, and another is said to have been a market gardener. When Peter and John were brought before the Council, they are spoken of as being, in a secular point of view, 'illiterate men, and of the lower sort,' and thus they are spoken of in a later age by the Fathers.

Inference and Assent in Religion   GA 467–8 (1870)

1   1 Cor 1, 26

My Brethren you know our Lord spoke, when He went away, of coming back, not only suddenly, but soon. Well, in the sense in which I have been speaking, He is ever coming. Again and again He comes to His Church; He ever comes as a strong warrior, bringing in with Him fresh and fresh captives of His arrows and His spear. That same marvel of an inward work in the souls of men on a large scale, which he wrought at the first, He is ever reiterating and renewing in the history of the Church down to this day. Multitudes are ever pouring into her, as the fish into Peter's net, beyond her own thought and her own act, by the immediate and secret operation of His grace.

Secret Power of Divine Grace   OS p. 55.   28th Pentecost, 1856

Fourth Sunday of the Year

Deut 18, 15–20; 1 Cor 7, 32–35; Mark 1, 21–28

Power over The Evil Spirits

And moreover let this too be observed, that on several occasions, the evil spirit, whom He was about to cast out, used towards our Lord the same phrase which He used towards His Mother. 'There was in their synagogue a man with an unclean spirit; and he cried out, saying, Let us alone; what have we to do with Thee, Thou Jesus of Nazareth? art Thou come to destroy us?' It is observable, too, that in another instance the devils alluded to the destined time. 'They cried out saying, What have we to do with Thee, Jesus, Thou Son of God? art Thou come hither to torment us *before the time*?' They knew a time was coming when He was to reign, and they to be punished; but they miscalculated it, and thought that because His work was not yet done, their torment was not yet to begin. And as when they said, 'What have we to do with Thee, before the time?' they implied that they should have to do with their Judge when the time came, and merely meant to say, 'What have we to do with Thee yet?'

Our Lord's Last Supper and His First   SD p. 35.   26 February, 1843

Accustom yourself to the idea, my brethren, and a terrible idea it is, that the state of sin is a demoniacal possession. Consider how such a possession of the body is spoken of in Scripture. Consider how the devil tormented the poor suffering body which he was allowed to get hold of. Then consider, what we may so often see now, what a fearful affliction madness is. Then, when you have considered these two things and got a clear hold of the idea, think that sin is just such a possession of the heart and spirit. It is not that the body is afflicted, as in the case of a demoniac. It is not that the reason is afflicted, as in the case of a madman. But it is that the spirit, the heart, the affections, the conscience, the will, are in the power of an evil spirit, who sways them about at his pleasure. How awful is this!

The World and Sin   CS p. 87.   2nd Lent.   19 March, 1848, St Chad's, Birmingham

Fifth Sunday of the Year

Job 7, 1–4. 6–7; 1 Cor 9, 16–19. 22–23; Mark 1, 29–39

'. . . they brought to him all who were sick'

Thus the Gospel, which has shed light in so many ways upon the state
of this world, has aided especially our view of the *sufferings* to which
human nature is subjected; turning a punishment into a privilege, in
the case of all pain, and especially of bodily pain, which is the most
mysterious of all. Sorrow, anxiety, and disappointment are more or
less connected with sin and sinners; but bodily pain is involuntary for
the most part, stretching over the world by some external irresistible
law, reaching to children who have never actually sinned, and to the
brute animals, who are strangers to Adam's nature, while in its
manifestations it is far more piteous and distressing than any other
suffering.

It is the lot of all of us, sooner or later; and that, perhaps in a
measure which it would be appalling and wrong to anticipate,
whether from disease, or from the casualties of life. And all of us at
length must die; and death is generally ushered in by disease, and ends
in that separation of soul and body, which itself may, in some cases,
involve peculiar pain.

Bodily Suffering   PPS III p. 142–3.   3 May, 1835

Sixth Sunday of the Year

Lev 13, 1–2. 44–46; 1 Cor 10, 31–11, 1; Mark 1, 40–45

The Cure of the Leper

Further; there is much in Elisha's miracles — nay, and in Elijah's in a degree — typical of the Christian sacraments. Naaman's cleansing in Jordan is a manifest figure of Holy Baptism, in which the leprosy of the soul is washed away by water. Again, the multiplying God's representative. Again; consider his conduct towards Naaman, which so grievously offended the proud Syrian. Instead of waiting upon him, he sent him a mere message to wash in Jordan. Thus he magnified his heavenly office, to remind Naaman that there was a God in Israel; whereas Naaman and his master had considered him a mere servant of the king of Israel, bound to do whatever he was bidden to do. Consider, too, his conduct to the messenger of Jehoram, already referred to, when he 'sat in his house and the elders with him'; and to Joash, on his death-bed, with whom 'the man of God was wroth,' because 'he smote thrice and stayed.'[1] What have we here but a figure of that Church to whom kings were to 'bow down with their face toward the earth, and lick up the dust of her feet'?[2]

Elisha a Type of Christ and His Followers SD p. 175. 178–9. 14 August, 1836

---

1   2 Kgs 5, 10; 6, 32. 33; 13, 14–19
2   Isa. 49, 23.

Seventh Sunday of the Year

Isa 43, 18–19. 21–22. 24–25; 2 Cor 1, 18–22; Mark 2, 1–12

'Who can forgive sins, but God?'

But the parable in the Gospel speaks of the time of evening, and by the evening is meant, not the end of the world, but the time of death. And really, perhaps, it will be as awful, though very different, that solitary judgement, when the soul stands before its Maker to answer for itself. Oh, who can tell which judgement is the more terrible – the silent secret judgement, or the open glorious coming of the judge. It will be most terrible certainly, and it comes first, to find ourselves by ourselves, one by one, in His presence, and to have brought before us most vividly all the thoughts, words, and deeds of this past life. Who will be able to bear the sight of himself? And yet we shall be obliged steadily to confront ourselves and to see ourselves. In this life we shrink from knowing our real selves. We do not like to know how sinful we are. We love those who prophesy smooth things to us, and we are angry with those who tell us of our faults. But then, not one fault only, but all the secret, as well evident, defects of our character will be clearly brought out. We shall see what we feared to see here, and much more. And then, when the full sight of ourselves comes to us, who will not wish that he had known more of himself here, rather than leaving it for the inevitable day to reveal it all to him!

I am speaking, not only of the bad but of the good. Those indeed who have died in neglect of good, it will be a most insufferably dreadful sight to them, and they will not have long to contemplate it in silence, for they will be hurried away to their punishment. But I speak of holy souls, souls that will be saved, and I say that to these the sight of themselves will be intolerable, and it will be a torment to them to see what they really are and the sins which lie against them. And hence some writers have said that their horror will be such that of their own will, and from a holy indignation against themselves, they will be ready to plunge into Purgatory in order to satisfy divine justice and to be clear of what is to their own clear sense and spiritual judgement so abominable. We do not know how great an evil sin is.

Preparation for the Judgement   CS p. 36–7.   20 February, 1848, St Chad's, Birmingham

But it may be asked, Did Christ hold out no hope for those who had lived in sin? Doubtless He did, if they determined to forsake their sin. He came to save all, whatever their former life, who gave themselves up to Him as their Lord and Saviour; and in His Church He gathered together of every kind, those who had departed from God, as well as those who had ever served Him well. Open sinners must have a beginning of repentance, if they are to repent; and on this first beginning Christ invites them to Him at once, without delay, for pardon and for aid. But this is not the question; of course all who come to Him will be received; none will be cast out. But the question is, not this, but whether they are likely to come, to hear His voice, and to follow Him; again whether they will, generally speaking, prove as consistent and deeply taught Christians as those who, compared with them, have never departed from God at all; and here all the advantage, doubtless, is on the side of those who (in the words of Scripture) have walked in the ordinances of the Lord blameless.[1] When sinners truly repent, then, indeed, they are altogether brothers in Christ's kingdom with those who have not in the same sense 'need of repentance'; but that they should repent at all is (alas!) so far from being likely, that when the unexpected event takes place it causes such joy in heaven (from the marvellousness of it) as is not even excited by the ninety and nine just persons who need no such change of mind.[2] Of such changes some instances are given us in the Gospels for the encouragement of all penitents, such as that of the woman, mentioned by St. Luke, who 'loved much'. Christ most graciously went among sinners, if so be He might save them; and we know that even those open sinners, when they knew that they were sinners, were nearer salvation, and in a better state, than the covetous and irreligious Pharisees, who added to their other gross sins, hypocrisy, blindness, a contempt of others, and a haughty and superstitious reliance on the availing virtue of their religious privileges.

Obedience to God the Way to Faith in Christ   PPS VIII p. 208–9.   31 October, 1830

1   Luke 1, 6.
2   Luke 15, 7.

Eighth Sunday of the Year

Hos 2, 16–17. 21–22; 2 Cor 3, 1–6; Mark 2, 18–22

The Power of Fasting

And this is another point which calls for distinct notice in the history of our Saviour's fasting and temptation, viz. the *victory* which attended it. He had three temptations, and thrice He conquered, – at the last He said, 'Get thee behind Me, Satan'; on which 'the devil leaveth Him.' This conflict and victory in the world unseen, is intimated in other passages of Scripture. The most remarkable of these is what our Lord says with reference to the demoniac, whom His Apostles could not cure. He had just descended from the Mount of Transfiguration, where, let it be observed, He seems to have gone up with His favoured Apostles to pass the night in prayer. He came down after that communion with the unseen world, and cast out the unclean spirit, and then He said, 'This kind can come forth by nothing but by prayer and fasting,'[1] which is nothing less than a plain declaration that such exercises give the soul power over the unseen world; nor can any sufficient reason be assigned for confining it to the first ages of the Gospel. And I think there is enough evidence, even in what may be known afterwards of the effects of such exercises upon persons now (not to have recourse to history), to show that these exercises are God's instruments for giving the Christian a high and royal power above and over his fellows.

Fasting a Source of Trial   PPS VI p. 10–11.   4 March, 1838

---

1   Mark 9, 29

Ninth Sunday of the Year

Deut 5, 12−15; 2 Cor 4, 6−11; Mark 2, 23−3, 6

The Lord of the Sabbath

The Jewish temple, the Jewish priesthood, and the Jewish sacrifices, then, were abolished because they were but shadows, and 'the body was of Christ'; but the precepts remain though the types disappear.

This, as I have already observed, is taught us in the chapter from which the text is taken, as is very plain. For instance, it tells us that the Sabbath is a shadow, and its observance not binding, since Christ is come, of whom is 'the body'. The Sabbath, according to St. Paul, is of the rudiments of this world, a carnal ordinance, and brings us into bondage. It had been a witness of the creation of heaven and earth, which was no longer needed. It was a memorial of past mercies to the Jews, which are surpassed in the Gospel. It was a type of the Gospel rest, which is now come. The type is fulfilled; the *whole* period of the Christian Church, from the day of Pentecost to the end of all things, is one holy and spiritual Sabbath. Again, the whole life of each individual Christian, from his baptism to his death, is also an antitype of the Jewish Sabbath.

The Principle of Continuity between the Jewish and Christian Church
SD p. 207−8.   20 November, 1842

It became one of the most binding of duties to hallow, i.e. to set apart the 7th day to an entire rest from all labour, as a sign of God's resting after creation — as the text says, 'the children of Israel shall keep the sabbath, to observe the sabbath throughout their generations' — again in the book of Leviticus 'Ye shall keep My sabbath, and reverence My sanctuary — I am the Lord' (Lev. 19,30) — And we may observe that the command is reiterated again and again (Exod. 16.29. Jer. 17,27. Ezek. 20,20) as if on purpose that they should by no possibility forget it. And in the 4th commandment it is said 'remember the sabbath' — as if to preclude all negligence — The keeping it was made a kind of test of keeping the whole law — because a person who broke the sabbath was in fact denying the fundamental principle of the law viz that Jehovah was Maker of heaven and earth — e.g. *'Blessed* is the man ... that keepeth the sabbath from polluting it...'

On the Sabbath as a Sign of the Creation to the Heathen   A.S.II p. 427.
19 March, 1826

Tenth Sunday of the Year

Gen 3, 9–15; 2 Cor 4, 13–5, 1; Mark 3, 20–35

The Sinless was called Beelzebul

There was a time when He wrought a miracle to convince the incredulous, but they had their ready explanation to destroy its cogency. 'There was offered unto Him,' says the Evangelist, 'one possessed with a devil, both blind and dumb; and He healed him, so that he both spoke and saw. And all the multitudes were amazed, and said, Is this not the son of David? But the Pharisees hearing it, said: *This man casteth not out devils but by Beelzebub, the prince of the devils.*' So said the Pharisees; and He of whom they spoke forewarned His disciples, that both He and His adversaries would have their respective representatives in after times, both in uttering and bearing a like blasphemy. 'The disciple is not above his master,' He said, 'nor the servant above his lord. It is enough for the disciple that he is as his master, and the servant as his lord. *If they have called the good-man of the house Beelzebub, how much more them of His household!*'

So it was, my Brethren, that our Saviour was not allowed to point to His miracles as His warrant, but was thought the worse of for them; and it cannot startle us that we too have to suffer the like in our day. The Sinless was called Beelzebub, much more His sinful servants. And what happened to Him then, is our protection as well as our warning now: for that must be a poor argument, which is available, not only against us, but against Him.

The world, then, witnesses, scrutinizes, and confesses the marvellousness of the Church's power. It does not deny that she is special, awful, nay, supernatural in her history; that she does what unaided man cannot do. It discerns and recognizes her abidingness, her unchangeableness, her imperturbability, her ever youthful vigour, the elasticity of her movements, the consistency and harmony of her teaching, the persuasiveness of her claims. It confesses, I say, that she is a supernatural phenomenon; but it makes short work with such a confession, viewed as an argument for submitting to her, for it ascribes the miracle which it beholds, to Satan, not to God.

Christ upon the Waters　OS 140. 141.　27 October, 1850

Eleventh Sunday of the Year

Ezek 17, 22–24; 2 Cor 5, 6–10; Mark 4, 26–34

'... as if a man should cast seed on the ground'

The truth has in itself the gift of spreading, without instruments; it makes its way in the world, under God's blessing, by its own persuasiveness and excellence; 'So is the kingdom of God,' says our Lord, 'as if a man should cast seed into the ground, and should sleep, and rise night and day, and the seed should spring and grow up, he *knoweth not* how.' The Word, when once uttered, runs its course. He who speaks it has done his work in uttering it, and cannot recall it if he would. It runs its course; it prospers in the thing whereunto God sends it. It seizes many souls at once, and subdues them to the obedience of faith. Now when bystanders see these effects and see no cause, for they will not believe that the Word itself is the cause, which is to them a dead-letter – when it sees many minds moved in one way in many places, it imputes to secret management that uniformity which is nothing but the echo of the One Living and True Word.

And of course all this happens to the surprise of Christians as well as of the world; they can but marvel and praise God, but cannot account for it more than the world. 'When the Lord turned again the captivity of Sion,' says the Psalmist, 'then were we like unto them that dream.'[1] Or as the Prophet says of the Church, 'Thine heart shall fear and be enlarged; because the abundance of the sea shall be converted unto thee, the forces of the Gentiles shall come unto thee,'[2] and here again the Christian's true wisdom looks like craft. It is true wisdom to leave the event to God; but when they are prospered, it looks like deceit to show surprise, and to disclaim the work themselves.

Wisdom and Innocence   SD 303–4.   19 February, 1843

1   Ps 126, 1 (*B.C.P.*)
2   Isa 60, 5

Twelfth Sunday of the Year

Job 38, 1. 8–11; 2 Cor 5, 14–17; Mark 4, 35–41

The Calming of the Storm

Our Lord commanded the winds and the sea, and the men who saw it marvelled, saying, What manner of man is this, for the winds and the sea obey him? It was a miracle. It showed our Lord's power over nature. And therefore they wondered, because they could not understand, and rightly, how any man could have power over nature, unless that power was given him by God. Nature goes on her own way and we cannot alter it. Man cannot alter it, he can only use it. Matter, for instance, falls downward; earth, stone, iron, all fall to the earth when left to themselves. Again, left to themselves, they cannot move except by falling. They never move except they are pulled or pushed forward. Water again never stands in a heap or a mass, but flows out on all sides as far as it can. Fire again always burns, or tends to burn. The wind blows to and fro, without any discoverable rule or law, and we cannot tell how it will blow tomorrow by seeing how it blows today. We see all these things. They have their own way. We cannot alter them. All we attempt to do is own purposes. Far different was it with our Lord: He used indeed the winds and the water (He used the water when He got into a boat, and used the wind when He suffered the sail to be spread over Him). He used, but more than this, He commanded, the winds and the waves – He had power to rebuke, to change, to undo the course of nature, as well as to make use of it. He was above nature. He had power over nature. This is what made the men marvel. Experienced seamen can make use of the winds and the waves to get to the shore. Nay, even in a storm they know how to avail themselves of them, they have their rules what to do, and they are on the look out.

No one has power over nature but He who made it. None can work a miracle but God. When miracles are wrought it is a proof that God is present. And therefore it is that, whenever God visits the earth, He works miracles. It is the claim He makes upon our attention. He thereby reminds us that He is the Creator. He who did, alone can undo. He who made, alone can destroy. He who gave nature its laws, alone can change those laws ...

He said to the disciples when the storm arose, 'Why are ye *fearful*?' That is, 'you ought to hope, you ought to trust, you ought to repose your heart on me. I am not only almighty, but I am all-merciful. I have come on earth because I am most loving to you. Why am I here, why am I in human flesh, why have I these hands which I stretch out to you, why have I these eyes from which the tears of pity flow, except that I wish you well, that I wish to save you? The storm cannot hurt you if *I* am with you. Can you be better placed than under My protection? Do you doubt My power or My will, do you think Me *negligent* of you that I sleep in the ship, and *unable* to help you except I am awake? Wherefore do you doubt? Wherefore do you fear? Have I been so long with you, and you do not yet trust Me and cannot remain in peace and quiet by My side?'

The Omnipotence of God, the Reason for Faith and Hope   CS p. 19–20, 21, 28–9, 30.   January, 1848. St Chad's, Birmingham

Thirteenth Sunday of the Year

Wisd 1, 13–15. 2, 23–24; 2 Cor 8, 7. 9. 13–15; Mark 5, 21–43

'Power went out of Him and healed all'

The woman with the issue of blood, who thought to be healed by secretly touching our Lord's garment, may perhaps be more correctly called superstitious than the barbarians of Melita. Yet it is remarkable that even she was encouraged by our Lord, and that on the very ground of her faith. In His judgement, then, a religious state of mind, which is not free from Superstition, may still be Faith, – nay, and high Faith. 'Daughter,' He said, 'be of good comfort; thy faith hath made thee whole; go in peace, and be whole of thy plague.' I have said that she showed a more superstitious temper than the people of Melita, inasmuch as what she did was inconsistent with what she knew. Her faith did not rise to the standard of her own light. She knew enough of the Good Shepherd to have directed her faith to Him as the one source of all good, instead of which she lingered in the circumstances and outskirts of His Divine Perfections. She in effect regarded the hem of His garment as an original principle of miraculous power, and thereby placed herself almost in the position of those who idolize the creature. Yet even this seems to have arisen from great humbleness of mind: like the servants of the ruler of the synagogue, who were then standing by, she feared probably to 'trouble the Master' with her direct intercession; or like the Apostles on a subsequent occasion, who rebuked those who brought children for His touch, she was unwilling to interrupt Him; or she was full of her own unworthiness, like the centurion who prayed that Christ would not condescend to enter his roof, but would speak the word instead, or send a messenger. She thought that a little one, such as herself, might come in for the crumbs from His table by chance, and without His distinct bidding, by the perpetual operation and spontaneous exuberance of those majestic general laws on which He wrought miracles. In all this, – in her faith and her humility, her faith tinged with superstition, her abject humility, – she would seem to resemble such worshippers in various ages and countries in the Christian Church, as have impaired their simple veneration of the Invisible, by an undue lingering of mind upon the outward emblems which they have considered He had blessed.

Love the Safeguard of Faith against Superstition US 244–6. 21 May, 1839

We are told on one occasion, 'the whole multitude sought to touch Him; for there went *virtue* out of Him, and healed them all.' Again, when the woman with the issue of blood touched Him, He 'immediately knew that virtue had gone out of Him.' Such grace was invisible, known only by the cure it effected, as in the case of the woman. Let us not doubt, though we do not sensibly approach Him, that He can still give us the virtue of His purity and incorruption, as He has promised, and in a more heavenly and spiritual manner, than 'in the days of His flesh'; in a way which does not remove the mere ailments of this temporal state, but sows the seed of eternal life in body and soul. Let us not deny Him the glory of His life-giving holiness, that diffusive grace which is the renovation of our whole race, a spirit quick and powerful and piercing, so as to leaven the whole mass of human corruption, and make it live. He is the first-fruits of the Resurrection: we follow Him each in his own order, as we are hallowed by His inward presence. And in this sense, among others, Christ, in the Scripture phrase, is 'formed in us'; that is, the communication is made to us of His new nature, which sanctifies the soul, and makes the body immortal.

Easter Day. Christ, a Quickening Spirit   PPS II p. 146—7.   3 April, 1831

Fourteenth Sunday of the Year

Ezek 2, 2–5; 2 Cor 12, 7–10; Mark 6, 1–6

A Prophet only despised in his own country

To all such arguments against religious truth, it is sufficient to reply, that no one who does not seek the truth with all his heart and strength, can tell what is of importance and what is not; that to attempt carelessly to decide on points of faith or morals is a matter of serious presumption; that no one knows *whither* he will be carried *if* he seeks the Truth perseveringly, and therefore, that since he cannot see at first starting the course into which his inquiries will be divinely directed, he *cannot* possibly say beforehand whether they may not lead him on to certainty as to things which at present he thinks trifling or extravagant or irrational ...

This is a subject which cannot too strongly be insisted on. Act up to your light, though in the midst of difficulties, and you will be carried on, you do not know how far. Abraham obeyed the call and journeyed, not knowing whither he went; so we, if we follow the voice of God, shall be brought on step by step into a new world, of which before we had no idea. This is His gracious way with us: He gives, not all at once, but by measure and season, wisely. To him that hath, more shall be given. But we must begin at the beginning. Each truth has its own order; we cannot join the way of life at any point of the course we please; we cannot learn advanced truths before we have learned primary ones. 'Call upon Me,' says the Divine Word, 'and I will answer thee, and show thee great and mighty things which though knowest not.'[1] Religious men are always learning; but when men refuse to profit by light already granted, their light is turned to darkness. Observe our Lord's conduct with the Pharisees. They asked him on what authority He acted. He gave them no direct answer, but referred them to the mission of John the Baptist – 'The baptism of John, whence was it? from heaven or from men?' They refused to say. Then He said, 'Neither tell I you by what authority I do these things.' That is, they would not profit by the knowledge they already had from St. John the Baptist, who spoke of Christ – therefore no more was given them.

Truth hidden when not sought after   PPS VIII p. 194–6.   17 October, 1830

1   Jer 33, 3

Fifteenth Sunday of the Year

Amos 7, 12–15; Eph 1, 3–14; Mark 6, 7–13

He sent them out with authority

Now, in the first place, as we all know, Christ chose twelve out of His disciples, whom He called Apostles, to be His representatives even during His own ministry. And He gave them the power of doing the wonderful works which He did Himself. Of course I do not say He gave them equal power (God forbid!); but He 'gave them power,' says St. Luke, 'and authority over all devils, and to cure diseases; and He sent them to preach the Kingdom of God, and to heal the sick.'[1] And He expressly made them His substitutes to the world at large; so that to receive them was to receive Himself. 'He that receiveth you, receiveth Me.'[2] Such was their principal power before His passion, similar to that which He principally exercised, viz. the commission to preach and to perform bodily cures. But when He had wrought out the Atonement for human sin upon the Cross, and purchased for man the gift of the Holy Ghost, then He gave them a higher commission; and still, be it observed, parallel to that which He Himself then assumed. '*As My Father hath sent Me, even so send I you*. And when He had said this, He breathed on them, and saith unto them, Receive ye the Holy Ghost. Whose soever sins ye remit, they are remitted unto them; and whose soever sins ye retain, they are retained.'[3] Here, then, the Apostles became Christ's representatives in the power of His Spirit, for the remission of sins, as before they were His representatives as regards miraculous cures, and preaching His Kingdom.

St. Peter The Christian Ministry   PPS II p. 301–2.   14 December, 1834

1   Luke 9, 1, 2.
2   Matt. 10. 40.
3   John, 20. 21–23.

Sixteenth Sunday of the Year

Jer 23, 1–6; Eph 2, 13–18; Mark 6, 30–34

'. . . like Sheep without a Shepherd'

'The good Shepherd giveth His life for the sheep.' In those countries of the East where our Lord appeared, the office of a shepherd is not only a lowly and simple-office, and an office of trust, as it is with us, but, moreover, an office of great hardship and of peril. Our flocks are exposed to no enemies, such as our Lord describes. The Shepherd here has no need to prove his fidelity to the sheep by encounters with fierce beasts of prey. The hireling shepherd is not tried. But where our Lord dwelt in the days of His flesh it was otherwise. There it was true that the good Shepherd giveth His life for the sheep – 'but he that is an hireling, and whose own the sheep are not, seeth the wolf coming, and leaveth the sheep, and fleeth, and the wolf catcheth them and scattereth the sheep. The hireling fleeth, because he is an hireling, and careth not for the sheep.'

   Our Lord found the sheep scattered; or, as He had said shortly before, 'All that ever came before Me are thieves and robbers'; and in consequence the sheep had no guide. Such were the priests and rulers of the Jews when Christ came; so that 'when He saw the multitudes He was moved with compassion on them, because they fainted, and were scattered abroad as sheep having no shepherd.'

The Shepherd of our Souls   PPS VIII p. 230–1.   30 April, 1843

Seventeenth Sunday of the Year

2 Kgs 4, 42–44; Eph 4, 1–6; John 6, 1–15

Bread in the Wilderness

And thus, throughout the course of His gracious dispensations from the beginning, it may be said that the Author and Finisher of our faith has hid things from us in mercy, and listened to our questionings, while He Himself knew what He was about to do. He has hid, in order afterwards to reveal, that then, on looking back on what He said and did before, we may see in it what at the time we did not see, and thereby see it to more profit. Thus He hid Himself from the disciples as He walked with them to Emmaus: thus Joseph, too, under different and yet similar circumstances, hid himself from his brethren.

With this thought in our minds, surely we seem to see a new and further meaning still, in the narrative before us. Christ spoke of buying bread, when he intended to create or make bread; but did He not, in that bread which He made, intend further that Heavenly bread which is the salvation of our souls? − for He goes on to say, 'Labour not for the meat' or food 'which perisheth, but for that food which endureth unto everlasting life, which the Son of man shall give unto you.' Yes, surely the wilderness is the world, and the Apostles are His priests, and the multitudes are His people; and that feast, so suddenly, so unexpectedly provided, is the Holy Communion. He alone is the same, He the provider of the loaves then, of the heavenly manna now. All other things change, but He remaineth.

The Gospel Feast   PPS VII p. 160–1.   20/27 May, 1838

Eighteenth Sunday of the Year

Exod 16, 2–4. 12–15; Eph 4, 17. 20–24; John 6, 24–35

'What Sign will you give us?'

There was another occasion on which the Jews asked for a sign, and on which our Lord answered by promising one, not to His Apostles only, but in continuance, like the manifestation He speaks of, to all His faithful followers. And it was a sign not more sensible or palpable, not less the object of faith as regards the many, than that sign of His resurrection which He gave once for all. He had just before been feeding five thousand men with five barley loaves and two small fishes; when, not contented with this, the Jews said, 'What sign showest Thou, that we may see and believe Thee? What dost Thou *work?*' and they proceeded to refer to the 'sign from heaven,' which Moses had given them. 'Our Fathers did eat manna in the desert, as it is written, He gave them bread from heaven to eat.' It was a little thing, they seemed to say, to multiply bread, but it was a great thing to send down bread from heaven, – a great thing, when the nature of the creature was changed, and men were made to live by the word of the Lord. Was the son of man able to give them bread such as this? Yes, surely, He had a Sign, – a Sign from heaven, more wonderful, a fearful Sign, surpassing thought and surpassing sight too, addressed to faith only, but not the less true because it was hidden. Moses gave their fathers bread from heaven; they saw it, ate it, and were dead; His sign was greater. He was Himself the Bread from heaven under the Gospel, and the Bread of life. He took not of the creature to satisfy their need, but He gave Himself for the life of the world. 'Moses gave you not that bread from heaven; but My Father giveth you the True Bread from heaven, for the Bread of God is He which cometh down from heaven and giveth life unto the world. I am the Bread of Life. This is the Bread which cometh down from heaven, that a man may eat thereof and not die.' Now I am not led to speak here of that special ordinance in which His Divine announcement is fulfilled; this would be foreign to my present purpose. I do but wish to consider the gift in itself, and the sign in itself, as these words describe it. It is a sign greater than manna, yet beyond dispute, as the passage itself shows, a sign not addressed to sight, but to faith. For our Lord speaks of our 'coming to Him,' and 'believing on Him'; and He says that 'it is the Spirit that quickeneth, the flesh profiteth nothing'; and He warns us, 'No one can come unto Me, except the Father which hath sent Me draw him.' His coming up from the heart of the earth was a sign for faith, not for sight; and such is His coming down from heaven as Bread.

The Gospel Sign addressed to Faith   PPS VI p. 110–11.   12/26 November, 1837

Nineteenth Sunday of the Year

1 Kgs 19, 4–8; Eph 4, 30–5, 2; John 6, 41–51

The True Bread from Heaven

Next, consider our Lord's allusion to the Manna. Persons there are who explain our eating Christ's flesh and blood, as merely meaning our receiving a *pledge* of the *effects* of the *passion* of His Body and Blood; that is, in other words, of the *favour* of Almighty God: but how can Christ's giving us His Body and Blood mean merely His giving us a pledge of His favour? Surely these awful words are far too clear and precise to be thus carelessly treated. Christ, as I have said, surely would not use such definite terms, did He intend to convey an idea so far removed from their meaning and so easy of expression in simple language. Now it increases the force of this consideration to observe that the manna, to which He compares His gift, was not a figure of speech, but a something definite and particular, really given, really received. The manna was not simply health, or life, or God's favour, but a certain something which caused health, continued life, and betokened God's favour. The manna was a gift external to the Israelites, and external also to God's own judgement of them and resolve concerning them, a gift created by Him and partaken by His people. And Christ, in like manner, says, that He Himself is to us the *true* Manna, the *true* Bread that came down from heaven; not like that manna which could not save its partakers from death, but a life-imparting manna. What therefore the manna was in the wilderness, that surely is the spiritual manna in the Christian Church; the manna in the wilderness was a real gift, taken and eaten; so is the manna in the Church. It is not God's mercy, or favour, or imputation; it is not a state of grace, or the promise of eternal life, or the privileges of the Gospel, or the new covenant; it is not, much less, the doctrine of the Gospel, or faith in that doctrine; but it is what our Lord says it is, the gift of His own precious Body and Blood, really given, taken, and eaten as the manna might be.

The Eucharistic Presence   PPS VI p. 143–4.   13 May, 1838

Twentieth Sunday of the Year

Prov 9, 1–6; Eph 5, 15–20; John 6, 51–58

His Life-giving Flesh

Why should this communion with Him be thought incredible, mysterious and sacred as it is, when we know from the Gospel how marvellously He wrought, in the days of His humiliation, towards those who approached Him? We are told on one occasion, 'the whole multitude sought to touch Him: for there went *virtue* out of Him, and healed them all.' Again, when the woman with the issue of blood touched Him, He 'Immediately knew that virtue had gone out of Him.'[1] Such grace was invisible, known only by the cure it effected, as in the case of the woman. Let us not doubt, though we do not sensibly approach Him, that He can still give us the virtue of His purity and incorruption, as He has promised, and in a more heavenly and spiritual manner, than 'in the days of His flesh'; in a way which does not remove the mere ailments of this temporal state, but sows the seed of eternal life in body and soul. Let us not deny Him the glory of His life-giving holiness, that diffusive grace which is the renovation of our whole race, a spirit quick and powerful and piercing, so as to leaven the whole mass of human corruption, and make it live. He is the first-fruits of the Resurrection: we follow Him each in his own order, as we are hallowed by His inward presence. And in this sense, among others, Christ, in the Scripture phrase, is 'formed in us';[2] that is, the communication is made to us of His new nature, which sanctifies the soul, and makes the body immortal.

Easter Day. Christ, a Quickening Spirit   PPS II p. 146–7.   3 April, 1831

---

1   Luke 6, 19; Mark 5, 30
2   Gal 4, 19

Twenty-first Sunday of the Year

Josh 24, 1–2. 15–18; Eph 5, 21–32; John 6, 60–69

'. . . For there are some of you who do not believe'

The Jews objected to our Lord, that He had said what was incredible, when He spoke of giving us His flesh. They 'strove among themselves, saying, How can this man give us His flesh to eat?' Our Saviour in answer, instead of retracting what He had said, spoke still more strongly – 'Except ye eat the flesh of the Son of man, and drink His blood, ye have no life in you.' But when they still murmured at it, and said, 'This is a hard saying, who can hear it?' – then He did in appearance withdraw His words. He said, 'It is the Spirit that quickeneth, the flesh profiteth nothing.' It would take us too long to enter now into the meaning of this declaration; but let us, for argument's sake, allow that He seems in them to qualify the wonderful words He had used at first; what follows from such an admission? This: – that our Lord acted according to His usual course on other occasions when persons refused His gracious announcements, not urging and insisting on them, but as if withdrawing them, and thus in one sense aiding those persons even in rejecting what they ought to have accepted without hesitation. This rule of God's dealings with unbelief, we find most fully exemplified in the instance of Pharaoh, whose heart God hardened because he himself hardened it. And so in this very chapter, as if in allusion to some such great law, He says, 'Murmur not among yourselves; No man can come to Me, except the Father which hath sent Me draw him'; as if He said, 'It is by a Divine gift that ye believe; beware, lest by objections you provoke God to take from you His aid, His preventing and enlightening grace.' And then, after they *had* complained, He did in consequence withdraw from them that gracious light which He had given, and spoke the words in question about the flesh and spirit, which would seem to carnal minds to unsay, or explain away, what He had said. But observe, He adds, 'There are some of you that believe not . . . *Therefore* said I unto you, that no man can come unto Me, except it were given unto Him of My Father.'

The Eucharistic Presence   PPS VI p. 148–149.   13 May, 1838

The most obvious answer, then, to the question why we yield to the authority of the Church in the questions and developments of faith, is, that some authority there must be if there is a revelation given, and other authority there is none but she. A revelation is not given, if there be no authority to decide what it is that is given. In the words of St. Peter to her Divine Master and Lord, 'To whom shall we go?' Nor must it be forgotten in confirmation, that Scripture expressly calls the Church 'the pillar and ground of the Truth.'[1]

Dev p. 88–89

---

1   1 Tim 3, 15

Twenty-second Sunday of the Year

Deut 4, 1–2. 6–8; Jas 1, 17–18. 21–22. 27; Mark 7, 1–8.
14–15. 21–23

Outward Observance

But supposing the objector supported what he said by Scripture:
supposing he said, for instance, that our Lord blamed persons who
washed their hands before eating bread, and that this proves that
washing the hands before a meal is wrong. I am taking no fictitious
case; such objections really have been made before now: yet the
answer surely is easy, namely, that our Saviour objected, not to the
mere washing of the hands, but to the making too much of such an
observance; to our thinking it religion, thinking that it would stand in
the stead of inward religion, and would make up for sins of the heart.
This is what He condemned, the show of great attention to outward
things, *while* inward things, which were more important, were
neglected. This, He says Himself, in His denunciation of the
Pharisees, 'These ought ye to have done,' He says, '*and not* to leave
the other,' the inward, '*undone.*' He says expressly they ought to do
the outward, but they ought to do more. They did the one and not the
other; they ought to have done both the one and the other.

Now, apply this to the case of beautifying Churches: – as is
neatness and decency in an individual, such is decoration in a Church;
and as we should be offended at slovenliness in an individual, so
ought we to be offended at disorder and neglect in our Churches. It
is quite true, men *are* so perverse (as the Pharisees were) that they
sometimes attend only to the outward forms, and neglect the inward
spirit; they may offer to Him costly furniture and goodly stones,
while they are cruel or bigoted; – just as persons may be neat in their
own persons and houses, and yet be ill-tempered and quarrelsome.
Or, again, they may carry their attention to the outward forms of
religion too far, and become superstitious; just as persons may carry
on a love of neatness into love of finery. And, moreover, Scripture
speaks against the hypocrisy of those who are religious outwardly,
while they live in sin, – just as it speaks against those who wash their
hands, while their heart is defiled. But still, in spite of all this,
propriety in appearance and dress is a virtue, – is next to godliness;
and, in like manner, decency and reverence are to be observed in the

worship of God, and are next to devotion, in spite of its being true that not all are holy who are grave and severe, not all devout who are munificent.

Offerings for the Sanctuary   PPS VI p. 301–2.   23 September, 1839

Twenty-third Sunday of the Year

Isa 35, 4–7; Jas 2, 1–5; Mark 7, 31–37

The Man who was deaf and dumb

Various maladies which our Lord cured, typical of various sins.

Blind. – Those that have not faith, and do not apprehend doctrine.

Deaf. – Those that are without devotion and cannot hear the songs of angels.

Dumb. – Those who through cowardice or pride do not confess the Gospel, though they believe in it.

Without taste (and smell)![1] – Those who have a dully unsensitive conscience.

Lame. – Those who are slothful.

SN p. 188.   31 July, 1864

---

1   alternative readings in the manuscript

... we too have miracles, but they are not outward but inward. Ours are not miracles of evidence, but of power and influence. They are secret, and more wonderful and efficacious because secret. Their miracles were wrought upon external nature; the sun stood still, and the sea parted. Ours are invisible, and are exercised upon the soul. They consist in the sacraments, and they just do that very thing which the Jewish miracles did not. They really touch the heart, though we so often resist their influence. If then we sin, as, alas! we do, if we do not love God more than the Jews did, if we have no heart for those 'good things which pass men's understanding,' we are not more excusable than they, but less so. For the supernatural works which God showed to them were wrought outwardly, not inwardly, and did not influence the will; they did but convey warnings; but the supernatural works which He does towards us are in the heart, and impart grace; and if we disobey, we are not disobeying His command only, but resisting His presence.

Miracles no Remedy for Unbelief   PPS VIII p. 86–7.   2 May, 1830

Twenty-fourth Sunday of the Year

Isa 50, 5–9; Jas 2, 14–18; Mark 8, 27–35

Peter's Faith

It would seem, then, that though Faith is the characteristic of the Gospel, and Faith is the simple lifting of the mind to the Unseen God, without conscious reasoning or formal argument, still the mind may be allowably, nay, religiously engaged, in reflecting upon its own Faith; investigating the grounds and the Object of it, bringing it out into words, whether to defend, or recommend, or teach it to others. And St. Peter himself, in spite of his ardour and earnestness, gives us in his own case some indications of such an exercise of mind. When he said, 'Thou art the Christ, the son of the Living God,' he cast his faith, in a measure, into a dogmatic form: and when he said, 'To whom shall we go? Thou hast the words of eternal life,' he gave 'an account of the hope that was in him,' or grounded his faith upon Evidence.

Implicit and Explicit Reason   US p. 253.   29 June, 1840

Twenty-fifth Sunday of the Year

Wisd 2, 12. 17—20; Jas 3, 16—4, 3; Mark 9, 30—37

... *Like Little Children*

If we wish to affect a person, and (if so be) humble him, what can we do better than appeal to the memory of times past, and above all to his childhood! Then it was that he came out of the hands of God, with all lessons and thoughts of Heaven freshly marked upon him ...

... The simplicity of a child's ways and notions, his ready belief of everything he is told, his artless love, his frank confidence, his confession of helplessness, his ignorance of evil, his inability to conceal his thoughts, his contentment, his prompt forgetfulness of trouble, his admiring without coveting; and, above all, his reverential spirit, looking at all things about him as wonderful, as tokens and types of the One Invisible, are all evidence of his being lately (as it were) a visitant in a higher state of things.

Holy Innocents. The Mind of Little Children PPS II p. 64, 65. 28 December, 1833

Humility or condescension, viewed as a virtue of conduct, may be said to consist, as in other things, so in our placing ourselves in our thoughts on a level with our inferiors; it is not only a voluntary relinquishment of the privileges of our own station, but an actual participation or assumption of the condition of those to whom we stoop. This is true humility, to feel and to behave as if we were low; not, to cherish a notion of our importance, while we affect a low position. Such was St. Paul's humility, when he called himself 'the least of the saints'; such the humility of those many holy men who have considered themselves the greatest of sinners. It is an abdication, as far as their own thoughts are concerned, of those prerogatives or privileges to which others deem them entitled. Now it is not a little instructive to contrast with this idea, Gentlemen, − with this theological meaning of the word 'condescension,' − its proper English sense; put them in juxta-position, and you will at once see the difference between the world's humility and the humility of the Gospel.

Knowledge and Religious Duty   Idea p. 205 (Discourse 8) 1852

Twenty-sixth Sunday of the Year

Num 11, 25–29; Jas 5, 1–6; Mark 9, 38–43. 45. 47–48

'Anyone who is not against us is for us'

Let it be observed, then, *who* it was who was not to be forbidden to use the Name of Jesus, though he did not follow the Apostles. Not one who preached *false* doctrine, not one who opposed the Apostles, or interfered with them, or had separated from them. Nothing then can be inferred from the test, – though we take it ever so literally, or apply it ever so exactly to the present times, – nothing, I repeat it, can be inferred in favour of those who separate from the Church, who set up against the Church, or who interfere with it, and trouble it. But there are a number of persons to whom the text does more or less apply, and whom we ought to treat according to its spirit. There are a number of persons not members of the Church, who neither have themselves separated from it, nor oppose it, nor usurp its place, but who are more or less in the condition of the man in the text, 'not following us,' yet using the Name of Jesus. Many sects and parties in this country are of long standing; many men are born in them; many men have had no opportunities of knowing the truth. Again, it may so happen they are exerting themselves for the cause of Christ in places where the Church is unknown, or where it does not extend itself. And, moreover, it may so be that they have upon them many consolatory proofs of seriousness and earnestness, of a true love for Christ, and desire to obey Him and not to magnify themselves. Here, then, our Lord seems to say, 'Forbid them not in their preaching.' ...

   On the whole, then, I would say this; when strangers to the Church preach great Christian truths, and do not oppose the Church, then, though we may not follow them, though we may not join them, yet we are not allowed to forbid them ...

The Fellowship of the Apostles   PPS VI p. 203–4, 205.   5 October, 1839

Twenty-seventh Sunday of the Year

Gen 2, 18–24; Heb 2, 9–11; Mark 10, 2–16

The Standard of Morality

Again, parents are bound to rebuke their children; but here the office is irksome for a different reason. It is misplaced affection, not fear, which interferes here with the performance of our duty. And besides, parents are indolent as well as overfond. They look to their home as a release from the world's cares, and cannot bear to make duties in a quarter where they would find a recreation. And they have their preferences and partialities about their children; and being alternately harsh and weakly indulgent, are not respected by them, even when they seasonably rebuke them.

And as to rebuke those who are inferior to us in the temporal appointments of Providence, is a serious work, so also, much more, does it require a ripeness in Christian holiness to rebuke our equals suitably; – and this, first, because we fear their ridicule and censure; next, because the failings of our equals commonly lie in the same line as our own, and every considerate person is aware, that, in rebuking another, he is binding himself to a strict and religious life, which we naturally shrink from doing. Accordingly, it has come to pass, that Christians, by a sort of tacit agreement, wink at each other's faults, and keep silence; whereas, if each of us forced himself to make his neighbour sensible when he did wrong, he would both benefit another, and, through God's blessing, would bind himself also to a more consistent profession. Who can say how much harm is done by thus countenancing the imperfections of our friends and equals? The standard of Christian morals is lowered; the service of God is mixed up with devotion to Mammon; and thus society is constantly tending to a heathen state. And this culpable toleration of vice is sanctioned by the manners of the present age, which seems to consider it a mark of good breeding not to be solicitous about the faith or conduct of those around us, as if their private views and habits were nothing to us; which would have more pretence of truth in it, were they merely our fellow-creatures, but is evidently false in the case of those who all the while profess to be Christians, who imagine that they gain the privileges of the Gospel by their profession, while they bring scandal on it by their lives.

Rebuking Sin   PPS II p. 296–7.   24 June, 1831

Twenty-eighth Sunday of the Year

Wisd 7, 7–11; Heb 4, 12–13; Mark 10, 17–30

The Rich Young Man

St. James says, 'Whosoever shall keep the whole law, and yet offend in one point, he is guilty of all.' And our Saviour assures us that 'Whosoever shall break one of these least commandments, and shall teach men so, he shall be called least in the kingdom of heaven'; and that 'Except our righteousness shall exceed the righteousness of the Scribes and Pharisees,' which was thus partial and circumscribed, 'we shall in no case enter into the kingdom of heaven.' And when the young man came to Him, saying that he had kept all the commandments, and asking what he lacked, He pointed out the 'one thing' wanting in him; and when he would not complete his obedience by that one thing, but went away sorrowful, then as if all his obedience in other points availed him nothing, Christ added, 'Children, how hard is it for them that trust in riches to enter into the Kingdom of God?' Let us not then deceive ourselves; what God demands of us is to fulfil His law, or at least to aim at fulfilling it; to be content with nothing short of perfect obedience, – to attempt everything, – to avail ourselves of the aids given us, and throw ourselves, not first, but afterwards on God's mercy for our short-comings. This is, I know, at first hearing a startling doctrine; and so averse are our hearts to it, that some men even attempt to maintain that it is an unchristian doctrine.

The Strictness of the Law of Christ   PPS IV p. 12.   9 July, 1837

1   Jas 2, 10. Matt. 5, 19, 20. Mark 10, 21, 24.

... The young ruler shrunk from the call, and found it a hard saying, 'If thou wilt be perfect, go and sell that thou hast, and give to the poor, and thou shalt have treasure in heaven; and come, and follow Me. But when the young man heard that saying, he went away sorrowful, for he had great possessions.' Others who seemed to waver, or rather who asked for some little delay from human feeling, were rebuked for want of promptitude in their obedience; − for time stays for no one; the word of call is spoken and is gone; if we do not seize the moment, it is lost.

Divine Calls.   PPS VIII p. 21.   27 October, 1839

Twenty-ninth Sunday of the Year

Isa 53, 10–11; Heb 4, 14–16; Mark 10, 35–45

The Need for Humility

You know well that the Gospel was at the first preached and propagated by the poor and lowly against the world's power; you know that fishermen and publicans overcame the world. You know it; you are fond of bringing it forward as an evidence of the truth of the Gospel, and of enlarging on it as something striking, and a topic for many words; happy are ye if yourselves fulfil it; happy are ye if *ye* carry on the work of those fishermen; if ye in your generation follow them as they followed Me, and triumph over the world and ascend above it by a like self-abasement.

Again, 'When thou art bidden of any man to a wedding, sit not down in the highest room; . . . but when thou art bidden, go and sit down in the lowest room, that when he that bade thee cometh, he may say unto thee, Friend, go up higher: then shalt thou have worship in the presence of them that sit at meat with thee; for whosoever exalteth himself shall be abased, and he that humbleth himself shall be exalted.' Here is a rule which extends to whatever we do. It is plain that the spirit of this command leads us, as a condition of being exalted hereafter, to cultivate here all kinds of little humiliations; instead of loving display, putting ourselves forward, seeking to be noticed, being loud or eager in speech, and bent on having our own way, to be content, nay, to rejoice in being made little of, to perform what to the flesh are servile offices, to think it enough to be barely suffered among men, to be patient under calumny; not to argue, not to judge, not to pronounce censures, unless a plain duty comes in; and all this because our Lord has said that such conduct is the very way to be exalted in His presence.

The Weapons of Saints   PPS VI p. 320–1.   29 October, 1837

Thirtieth Sunday of the Year

Jer 31, 7–9; Heb 5, 1–6; Mark 10, 46–52

'Master, let me see'

To know God and Christ, in Scripture language, seems to mean to live under the conviction of His presence, who is to our bodily eyes unseen. It is, in fact, to have faith, according to St. Paul's account of faith, as the substance and evidence of what is invisible. It is faith, but not faith such as a Heathen might have, but Gospel faith; for only in the Gospel has God so revealed Himself, as to allow of that kind of faith which may be called, in a special manner, knowledge. The faith of Heathens was *blind*; it was more or less a moving forward in the darkness, with hand and foot; – therefore the Apostle says, 'if haply they might *feel* after Him.'[1] But the Gospel is a *manifestation*, and therefore addressed to the eyes of our mind. Faith is the same principle as before, but with the opportunity of acting through a more certain and satisfactory sense. We recognise objects by the eye at once; but not by the touch. We know them when we see them, but scarcely till then. Hence it is, that the New Testament says so much on the subject of spiritual knowledge. For instance, St. Paul prays that the Ephesians may receive 'the spirit of wisdom and revelation in the knowledge of Christ, the eyes of their understanding being enlightened';[2]

Saving Knowledge PPS II p. 151–2. Jan/Feb 1835

1 Acts 17, 27
2 Eph 1, 18

When His word and His outward world are at variance in the information they convey to us, it is our bounden duty to trust the revealed word, and not the visible world. Not that sight is not His gift, but that He has demanded of us as Christians, as a sort of poor return for His love to us, that when these two informants, one natural, the other revealed, oppose each other, we should trust for a little while the latter, − for a little while, till this world of shadows passes away, and we find ourselves in that new world, in which there is no contradiction between sight and hearing, but absolute unity and harmony in all things, for He is the light of it. But till then, it is our very profession, as children of the kingdom, to walk by faith not by sight.

Faith and Experience   SD p. 64.   25 November, 1838

Thirty-first Sunday of the Year

Deut 6, 2–6; Heb 7, 23–28; Mark 12, 28–34

Loving one's neighbour

We have not seen God. How are we to ascertain that we love Him? Feelings are deceptive. Thus, as by a test, by loving others, by love of man. And so St. John says, 1 John 4, 12.

First, we should love man *merely* as the work of God. If we love God, we shall love all His works. Undevout men walk about, and look round, and they never associate what they see with God; but everything is the work of God.

Love of our neighbour   SN p. 133.   7 September, 1856

The answer of the scribe, which our blessed Lord here commends, was occasioned by Christ's setting before him the two great commandments of the Law. When He had declared the love of God and of man to comprehend our whole duty, the scribe said, 'Master, Thou hast said the truth: for there is one God; and there is none other but He: and to love Him with all the heart, and with all the understanding, and with all the soul, and with all the strength, and to love his neighbour as himself, is more than all whole burnt-offerings and sacrifices.' Upon this acknowledgement of the duty of general religious obedience, Christ replied, in the words of the test, 'Thou art not far from the kingdom of God,' i.e. Thou art not far from being a Christian.

In these words, then, we are taught, first, that the Christian's faith and obedience are not the same religion as that of natural conscience, as being some way beyond it; secondly, that this way is 'not far,' not far in the case of those who try to act up to their conscience; in other words, that obedience to conscience leads to obedience to the Gospel, which, instead of being something different altogether, is but the completion and perfection of that religion which natural conscience teaches.

Indeed, it would have been strange if the God of nature had said one thing, and the God of grace another; if the truths which our conscience taught us without the information of Scripture, were contradicted by that information when obtained. But it is not so; there are not two ways of pleasing God; what conscience suggests, Christ has sanctioned and explained; to love God and our neighbour are the great duties of the Gospel as well as of the Law; he who endeavours to fulfil them by the light of nature is in the way towards, is, as our Lord said, 'not far from Christ's kingdom'; for to him that hath more shall be given.

Obedience to God the Way to Faith in Christ   PPS VIII p. 201–2.   31 October, 1830

Thirty-second Sunday of the Year

1 Kgs 17, 10–16; Heb 9, 24–28; Mark 12, 38–44

True Detachment

Detachment, as we know from spiritual books, is a rare and high Christian virtue; a great Saint, St. Philip Neri, said that, if he had a dozen really detached men, he should be able to convert the world. To be detached is to be loosened from every tie which binds the soul to the earth, to be dependent on nothing sublunary, to lean on nothing temporal; it is to care simply nothing what other men choose to think or say of us, or do to us; to go about our own work, because it is our duty, as soldiers go to battle, without a care for the consequences; to account credit, honour, name, easy circumstances, comfort, human affections, just nothing at all, when any religious obligation involves the sacrifice of them. It is to be as reckless of all these goods of life on such occasions, as under ordinary circumstances we are lavish and wanton, if I must take an example, in our use of water, – or as we make a present of our words without grudging to friend or stranger, – or as we get rid of wasps or flies or gnats, which trouble us, without any sort of compunction, without hesitation before the act, and without a second thought after it.

HS III p. 130 (1854)

Man has confidence in man, he trusts to the credit of his neighbour; but Christians do not risk largely upon their Saviour's word; and this is the one thing they have to do. Christ tells us Himself, 'Make to yourselves friends of the mammon of unrighteousness; that, when ye fail, they may receive you into everlasting habitations';[1] i.e. buy an interest in the next world with that wealth which this world uses unrighteously; feed the hungry, clothe the naked, relieve the sick, and it shall turn to 'bags that wax not old, a treasure in the heavens that faileth not.' Thus almsdeeds, I say, are an intelligible venture, and an evidence of faith.

So again the man who, when his prospects in the world are good, gives up the promise of wealth or of eminence, in order to be nearer Christ, to have a place in His temple, to have more opportunity for prayer and praise, he makes a sacrifice.

The Ventures of Faith   PPS IV p. 302–3.   21 February, 1836

---

1   Luke 16. 9.

Thirty-third Sunday of the Year

Dan 12, 1–3; Heb 10, 11–14. 18; Mark 13, 24–32

The Signs of the End

I have two remarks to add: first, that it is quite certain, that if such a persecution has been foretold, it has not yet come, and therefore is to come. We may be wrong in thinking that Scripture foretells it, though it has been the common belief, I may say, of all ages; but if there be a persecution, it is still future. So that every generation of Christians should be on the watch-tower, looking out, – nay, more and more, as time goes on.

Next, I observe that signs do occur from time to time, not to enable us to fix the day, for that is hidden, but to show us it is coming. The world grows old – the earth is crumbling away – the night is far spent – the day is at hand. The shadows begin to move – the old forms of empire, which have lasted ever since our Lord was with us, heave and tremble before our eyes, and nod to their fall. These it is that keep Him from us – He is behind them. When they go, Antichrist will be released from 'that which withholdeth,'[1] and after his short but fearful season, Christ will come.

The Persecution of Antichrist   DA p. 102–3 (Tract 85, 21 September, 1838)

---

1   2 Thess 2, 6

Our Lord Jesus Christ, Universal King (34th Sunday)

Dan 7, 13 – 14; Rev 1, 5 – 8; John 18, 33 – 37

A Witness to the Truth

This sense of the seriousness of our charge is increased by considering, that after all we do not know, and cannot form a notion, what is the real final object of the Gospel Revelation. Men are accustomed to say, that it is the salvation of the world, which it certainly is not. If, instead of this, we say that Christ came 'to purify unto Himself a peculiar people,' then, indeed, we speak a great Truth; but this, though a main end of our preaching, is not its simple and ultimate object. Rather, as far as we are told at all, that object is the glory of God; but we cannot understand what is meant by this, or how the Dispensation of the Gospel promotes it. It is enough for us that we must act with the simple thought of God before us, make all ends subordinate to this, and leave the event to Him. We know, indeed, to our great comfort, that we cannot preach in vain. His heavenly word 'shall not return unto Him void, but shall prosper in the thing whereto He sent it.'[1] Still it is surely our duty to preach, 'whether men will hear, or whether they will forbear.'[2] We must preach, as our Lord enjoins in a text already quoted, 'as a witness.' Accordingly He Himself, before the heathen Pilate, 'bore witness unto the truth' ...

Trinity Sunday. The Gospel, A Trust committed to us   PPS II p. 267.   Nov/Dec 1834

---

1   Isa 55, 11
2   Ezek 2, 5. 7

First Sunday of Advent

Jer 33, 14−16; 1 Thess 3, 12−4, 2; Luke 21, 25−28. 34−36

Signs in the Heavens

One day the lights of heaven *will* be signs; one day the affairs of nations also *will* be signs; why, then, is it superstitious to *look* towards them? It is not. We may be wrong in the particulars we rest upon, and may show our ignorance in doing so; but there is nothing ridiculous or contemptible in our ignorance, and there is much that is religious in our watching. It is better to be wrong in our watching, than not to watch at all.

Nor does it follow that Christians were wrong, even in their particular anticipations, though Christ did not come, whereas they said, they saw His signs. Perhaps they were His signs, and He withdrew them again. Is there no such thing as countermanding? Do not skilful men in matters of this world sometimes form anticipations which turn out wrong, and yet we say that they ought to have been right? The sky threatens and then clears again. Or some military leader orders his men forward, and then for some reason recalls them; shall we say that informants were wrong who brought the news that he was moving? Well, in one sense Christ is ever moving forward, ever checking, the armies of heaven. Signs of the white horses are ever appearing, ever vanishing.[1] 'Clouds return after the rain'; and His servants are not wrong in pointing to them, and saying that the weather is breaking, though it does not break, for it is ever unsettled.

And another thing should be observed, that though Christians have ever been expecting Christ, ever pointing to His signs, they have never said that He was come. They have but said that He was just coming, *all but* come. And so He was and is. Enthusiasts, sectaries, wild presumptuous men, *they* have said that He was *actually* come, or they have pointed out the exact year and day in which He would come. Not so His humble followers. They have neither announced nor sought Him, either in the desert or in the secret chambers, nor have they attempted to determine 'the times and seasons, which the Father has put in His own power.' They have but waited; when He actually comes, they will not mistake Him; and before then, they pronounce nothing. They do but see His forerunners.

Waiting for Christ PPS VI p. 246−7.   29 November and 6 December, 1840

1   Rev 6, 2f

Second Sunday of Advent

Baruch 5, 1–9; Phil 1, 4–6. 8–11; Luke 3, 1–6

A Voice cries in the Wilderness

The Holy Baptist was sent before our Lord to prepare His way; that is, to be His instrument in rousing, warning, humbling, and inflaming the hearts of men, so that, when He came, they might believe in Him. He Himself is the Author and Finisher of that Faith, of which He is also the Object; but, ordinarily, He does not implant it in us suddenly, but He first creates certain dispositions, and these He carries on to faith as their reward. When then He was about to appear on earth among His chosen people, and to claim for Himself their faith, He made use of St. John first to create in them these necessary dispositions.

   Now these passages cannot mean that faith is against reason, or that reason does not ordinarily precede faith, for this is a doctrine quite contrary to Revelation, but I think I shall not be wrong in understanding them thus, – that with good dispositions faith *is* easy; and that without good dispositions, faith is *not* easy; and that those who were praised for their faith, were such as had already the good dispositions, and that those who were blamed for their unbelief, were such as were wanting in this respect, and would have believed, or believed sooner, had they possessed the necessary dispositions for believing, or a greater share of them. This is the point I am going to insist on: I am led to it by the Baptist's especial office of 'preparing the way of the Lord'; for by that preparation is meant the creating in the hearts of his hearers the dispositions necessary for faith. And I consider that the same truth is implied in the glorious hymn of the Angels upon Christmas night; for to whom was the Prince of Peace to come? They sang, 'Glory to God in the highest, and on earth *peace to men of good will*.' By 'good will' is meant, 'good disposition'; the peace of the Gospel, the full gifts of the knowledge, and of the power, and of the consolation of Christian Redemption, were to be the reward of men of *good dispositions. They* were the men to whom the Infant Saviour came; *they* were those in whom His grace would find its fruit and recompense; *they* were those, who, by congruous merit, would be led on, as the Evangelist says, to '*believe* in His Name,' and 'to be born, not of blood, nor of the will of the flesh, nor of the will of man, but of God.'

Dispositions for Faith   OS p. 60. 63.   4th Advent, 1856

Third Sunday of Advent

Zech 3, 14–18; Phil 1, 4–7; Luke 3, 10–18

He is All Holy, yet I come before Him

But once more. You ask, how you can make up your mind to stand before your Lord and God; I ask in turn, how do you bring yourself to come before Him now day by day? – for what is this but meeting Him? Consider what it is you mean by praying, and you will see that, at that very time that you are asking for the coming of His kingdom you are anticipating that coming, and accomplishing the thing you fear. When you pray, you come into His presence. Now reflect on yourself, what your feelings are in coming. They are these: you seem to say, – I am in myself nothing but a sinner, a man of unclean lips and earthly heart. I am not worthy to enter into His presence. I am not worthy of the least of all His mercies. I know He is All-holy, yet I come before Him; I place myself under His pure and piercing eyes, which look me through and through, and discern every trace and every motion of evil within me. Why do I do so? First of all, for this reason. To whom should I go? What can I do better? Who is there in the whole world that can help me? Who that will care for me, or pity me, or have any kind thought of me, if I cannot obtain it of Him? I know He is of purer eyes than to behold iniquity; but I know again that He is All-merciful, and that He so sincerely desires my salvation that He has died for me. Therefore, though I am in a great strait, I will rather fall into His hands, than into those of any creature. True it is I could find creatures more like myself, imperfect or sinful; it might seem better to betake myself to some of these who have power with God, and to beseech them to interest themselves for me. But no; somehow I cannot content myself with this; – no, terrible as it is, I had rather go to God alone. I have an instinct within me which leads me to rise and go to my Father, to name the Name of His well-beloved Son, and having named it, to place myself unreservedly in His hands, saying, 'If Thou, Lord, wilt be extreme to mark what is done amiss, O Lord, who may abide it? But there is forgiveness with Thee.'[1] – This is the feeling in which we come to confess our sins, and to pray to God for pardon and grace day by day.

Shrinking from Christ's Coming   PPS V p. 54–5.   4 December, 1836

1   Ps 130, 3. 4 (*B.C.P.*)

Fourth Sunday of Advent

Mic 5, 1–4; Heb 10, 5–10; Luke 1, 39–45

Hail, Full of Grace

All generations have called her blessed. The Angel began the salutation; he said, 'Hail, thou that art highly favoured; the Lord is with thee; blessed art thou among women.' Again he said, 'Fear not, Mary, for thou hast found favour with God; and, behold, thou shalt conceive in thy womb, and bring forth a Son, and shalt call His name Jesus. He shall be great, and shall be called the Son of the Highest.' Her cousin Elizabeth was the next to greet her with her appropriate title. Though she was filled with the Holy Ghost at the time she spake, yet, far from thinking herself by such a gift equalled to Mary, she was thereby moved to use the lowlier and more reverent language. 'She spake out with a loud voice, and said, *Blessed art thou* among women, and blessed is the fruit of thy womb. And whence is this to me, that the mother of my Lord should come to me?' ... Then she repeated, 'Blessed is she that believed; for there shall be a performance of those things which were told her from the Lord.' Then it was that Mary gave utterance to her feelings in the Hymn which we read in the Evening Service.[1] How many and complicated must they have been! In her was now to be fulfilled that promise which the world had been looking out for during thousands of years. The Seed of the woman, announced to guilty Eve, after long delay, was at length appearing upon earth, and was to be born of her. In her the destinies of the world were to be reversed, and the serpent's head bruised. On her was bestowed the greatest honour ever put upon any individual of our fallen race. God was taking upon Him her flesh, and humbling Himself to be called her off-spring; – such is the deep mystery! She of course would feel her own inexpressible unworthiness; and again her humble lot, her ignorance, her weakness in the eyes of the world. And she had moreover, we may well suppose, that purity and innocence of heart, that bright vision of faith, that confiding trust in her God, which raised all these feelings to an intensity which we, ordinary mortals, cannot understand. *We* cannot understand them; we repeat her hymn day after day, – yet consider for an instant in how different a mode *we* say it from that in which she at first uttered it.

Annunciation of the Blessed Virgin. The Reverence due to Her   PPS II p. 127–8
25 March, 1832

Christmastide – as for Year A

1   The *Magnificat*

Sunday in the Octave of Christmas: The Holy Family

1 Sam 1, 20–22. 24–28; 1 John 3, 1–2. 21–24; Luke 2, 41–52

Mary, our Pattern of Faith

But Mary's faith did not end in a mere acquiescence in Divine providences and revelations; as the text informs us, she 'pondered' them. When the shepherds came, and told of the vision of the Angels which they had seen at the time of the Nativity, and how one of them announced that the Infant in her arms was 'the Saviour, which is Christ the Lord,' while others did but wonder, 'Mary kept all these things, and pondered them in her heart.' Again, when her Son and Saviour had come to the age of twelve years, and had left her for awhile for His Father's service, and had been found, to her surprise, in the Temple, amid the doctors, both hearing them and asking them questions, and had, on her addressing Him, vouchsafed to justify His conduct, we are told, 'His mother kept all these sayings in her heart.' And accordingly, at the marriage-feast in Cana, her faith anticipated His first miracle, and she said to the servants, 'Whatsoever He saith unto you, do it.'

Thus, St. Mary is our pattern of Faith, both in the reception and in the study of Divine Truth. She does not think it enough to accept, she dwells upon it; not enough to possess, she uses it; not enough to assent, she develops it; not enough to submit the Reason, she reasons upon it; not indeed reasoning first, and believing afterwards, with Zacharias, yet first believing without reasoning, next from love and reverence, reasoning after believing.

The Theory of Developments   US p. 312–3.   2 February, 1843

January 1st, Epiphany and 2nd Sunday after Christmas – as for Year A

The Baptism of the Lord (First Sunday after Epiphany)

Isa 40, 1–5. 9–11; Tit 2, 11–14. 3, 4–7; Luke 3, 15–16. 21–22

The Grace of our Baptism

The Apostles then, standing in Christ's place, were consequently exalted by office far above any divine Messengers before them. We come to the same conclusion from considering the sacred treasures committed to their custody, which (not to mention their miraculous powers, which is beside our present purpose) were those peculiar spiritual blessings which flow from Christ as a Saviour, as a Prophet, Priest, and King.

These blessings are commonly designated in Scripture as 'the Spirit,' or 'the gift of the Holy Ghost.' John the Baptist said of himself and Christ; 'I indeed baptize you with water unto repentance; but He shall baptize you with the Holy Ghost, and with fire.'

St Peter. The Christian Ministry PPS II p. 302–3. 14 December, 1834

First Sunday of Lent

Deut 26, 4–10; Rom 10, 8–13; Luke 4, 1–13

Victory in Trial

And this is another point which calls for distinct notice in the history of our Saviour's fasting and temptation, viz. the *victory* which attended it. He had three temptations, and thrice He conquered, – at the last He said, 'Get thee behind Me, Satan'; on which 'the devil leaveth Him.' This conflict and victory in the world unseen, is intimated in other passages of Scripture. The most remarkable of these is what our Lord says with reference to the demoniac, whom His Apostles could not cure. He had just descended from the Mount of Transfiguration, where, let it be observed, He seems to have gone up with His favoured Apostles to pass the night in prayer. He came down after that communion with the unseen world, and cast out the unclean spirit, and then He said, 'This kind can come forth by nothing but by prayer and fasting,'[1] which is nothing less than a plain declaration that such exercises give the soul power over the unseen world; nor can any sufficient reason be assigned for confining it to the first ages of the Gospel. And I think there is enough evidence, even in what may be known afterwards of the effects of such exercises upon persons now (not to have recourse to history), to show that these exercises are God's instruments for giving the Christian a high and royal power above and over his fellows.

Fasting a Source of Trial   PPS VI p. 10–11.   4 March, 1838

---

1   Mark 9, 29.

Second Sunday of Lent

Gen 15, 5 – 12. 17 – 18; Phil 3, 17 – 4, 1; Luke 9, 28 – 36

Moses and Elijah appeared with him . . .

Consider, for instance, how the prospect of our Lord's passion opens upon the Apostles in the sacred history. Where did they hear of it? 'Moses and Elias on the mountain appeared with Him in glory, and spake of His decease, which He should accomplish at Jerusalem.'[1] That is, the season of His bitter trial was preceded by a short gleam of the glory which was to be, when He was suddenly transfigured, 'and the fashion of His countenance was altered, and His raiment was white and glistering.'[2] And with this glory in prospect, our Lord abhorred not to die: as it is written, 'Who for the joy that was set before Him, endured the Cross, despising the shame.'[3]

Again, He forewarned His Apostles that they in like manner should be persecuted for righteousness' sake, and be afflicted and delivered up, and hated and killed. Such was to be their life in this world, 'that if in this world only they had had hope in Christ, they had been of all men most miserable.'[4] Well then, observe, their trial too was preceded by a season of peace and pleasantness, in anticipation of their future reward; for before the day of Pentecost, for forty days Christ was with them, soothing, comforting, confirming them, 'and speaking of the things pertaining unto the kingdom of God.'[5] As Moses stood on the Mount and saw the promised land and all its riches, and yet Joshua had to fight many battles before he got possession, so did the Apostles, before descending into the valley of the shadow of death, whence nought of heaven was to be seen, stand upon the heights, and look over that valley, which they had to cross, to the city of the living God beyond it.

The Season of Epiphany PPS VII p. 81 – 2. 17 January, 1841

1 Luke 9, 30. 31
2 Luke 9, 29
3 Heb 12, 2
4 1 Cor 15, 19
5 Acts 1, 3

Cf. Feast of The Transfiguration

Third Sunday of Lent

Exod 3, 1–8. 13–15; 1 Cor 10, 1–6. 10–12; Luke 13, 1–9

'Unless you repent ...'

For you were once sinners; either by open and avowed contempt of religion, or by secret transgression, or by carelessness and coldness, or by some indulged bad habit, or by setting your heart on some object of this world, and doing your own will instead of God's, I think I may say you have needed, or now need a reconciliation to Him. You have needed, or you need, to be brought near to Him, and to have your sins washed away in His blood, and your pardon recorded in Heaven. And what will do this for you, but contrition? and what is contrition without love? I do not say that you must have the love which Saints have, in order to obtain your forgiveness, the love of St. Peter or of St. Mary Magdalen; but still without your portion of that same heavenly grace, how can you be forgiven at all? If you would do works meet for penance, they must proceed from a living flame of charity. If you would secure perseverance to the end, you must gain it by continual loving prayer to the Author and Finisher of faith and obedience.

Purity and Love   Mix p. 79–80 (Discourse 4) 1849

But, after all, there are very many more than I have as yet mentioned, who wait for a time of repentance to come while at present they live in sin. For instance, the young, who consider it will be time enough to think of God when they grow old; that religion will then come as a matter of course, and that they will then like it naturally, just as they now like their follies and sins. Or those who are much engaged in worldly business, who confess they do not give that attention to religion which they ought to give; who neglect the ordinances of the Church; who desecrate the Lord's day; who give little or no time to the study of God's word; who allow themselves in various small transgressions of their conscience, and resolutely harden themselves against the remorse which such transgressions are calculated to cause them; and all this they do under the idea that at length a convenient season will come when they may give themselves to religious duties. They determine on retiring at length from the world, and of making up for lost time by greater diligence then. All such persons, and how many they are! think that they will be able to seek Christ when they please, though they have lived all their lives with no true love either of God or man; i.e. they do not, in their hearts, believe our Lord's doctrine contained in the text, that to obey God is to be near Christ, and that to disobey is to be far from Him.

Obedience to God the Way to Faith in Christ.   PPS VIII p. 213–4.   31 October, 1830

Fourth Sunday of Lent

Josh 5, 9–12; 2 Cor 5, 17–21; Luke 15, 1–3. 11–32

The prodigal son

We are ever sinning, we must ever be renewing our sorrow and our purpose of obedience, repeating our confessions and our prayers for pardon. No need to look back to the first beginnings of our repentance, should we be able to trace these, as something solitary and peculiar in our religious course; we are *ever* but beginning; the most perfect Christian is to himself but a beginner, a penitent prodigal, who has squandered God's gifts, and comes to Him to be tried over again, not as a son, but as a hired servant.

In this parable, then, we need not understand the description of the returning prodigal to imply that there is a state of disobedience and subsequent state of conversion definitely marked in the life of Christians generally. It describes the state of all Christians at all times, and is fulfilled more or less, according to circumstances, in this case or that; fulfilled in one way and measure at the beginning of our Christian course, and in another at the end. So I shall now consider it, viz., as describing the *nature* of all true repentance.

First, observe, the prodigal son said, 'I am no more worthy to be called Thy son, make me as one of Thy hired servants.' We know that God's service is perfect freedom, not a servitude; but this it is in the case of those who have long served Him; at first it *is* a kind of servitude, it is a task till our likings and tastes come to be in unison with those which God has sanctioned.

Now, I insist upon this, because the conscience of a repentant sinner is often uneasy at finding religion a task to him. He thinks he ought to rejoice in the Lord at once, and it is true he is often told to do so; he is often taught to begin by cultivating high affections. Perhaps he is even warned against offering to God what is termed a *formal service*. Now this is reversing the course of a Christian's life. The prodigal son judged better, when he begged to be made one of his father's servants – he knew his place. We *must begin* religion with what looks like a form. Our fault will be, not in beginning it as a form, but in continuing it as a form. For it is our duty to be ever striving and praying to enter into the real spirit of our services, and in proportion as we understand them and love them, they will cease to be a form and a task, and will be the real expressions of our minds. Thus shall we gradually be changed in heart from servants into sons of Almighty God.

Christian Repentance   PPS III p. 91–2. 93–4.   20 November, 1831

Cf. 24th Sunday of the Year (C)

Fifth Sunday of Lent

Isa 43, 16−21; Phil 3, 8−14; John 8, 1−11

Confession of Sin

Therefore let a man reflect, whoever from tenderness of conscience shuns the Church as above him (whether he shuns her services, or her sacraments), that, awful as it is to approach Christ, to speak to Him, to 'eat His flesh and drink His blood,' and to live in Him, *to whom shall he go*? See what it comes to. Christ is the only way of salvation open to sinners. Truly we *are* children, and cannot suitably feel the words which the Church teaches us, though we say them after her, nor feel duly reverent at God's presence! Yet let us but know our own ignorance and weakness, and we are safe. God accepts those who thus come in faith, bringing nothing as their offering, but a confession of sin. And this is the highest excellence to which we ordinarily attain; to understand our own hypocrisy, insincerity, and shallowness of mind, − to own, while we pray, that we cannot pray aright, − to repent of our repentings, − and to submit ourselves wholly to His judgment, who could indeed be extreme with us, but has already shown His loving-kindness in bidding us to pray. And, while we thus conduct ourselves, we must learn to feel that God knows all this before we say it, and far better than we do. He does not need to be informed of our extreme worthlessness. We must pray in the spirit and the temper of the extremest abasement, but we need not search for adequate words to express this, for in truth no words are bad enough for our case. Some men are dissatisfied with the confessions of sin we make in Church, as not being strong enough; but none *can* be strong enough; let us be satisfied with sober words, which have been ever in use; it will be a great thing if we enter into *them*. No need of searching for impassioned words to express our repentance, when we do not rightly enter even into the most ordinary expressions.

Profession without Hypocrisy   PPS I p. 146−7.   23 October, 1831

Passion Sunday (Palm Sunday)

Isa 50, 4–7; Phil 2, 6–11; Luke 22, 14–23. 56

He was crucified also for us

'The Word became flesh': even this would seem mystery and marvel enough, but even this was not all; not only was He 'made man,' but, as the Creed goes on to state, He 'was crucified also for us under Pontius Pilate, He suffered and was buried.'

Now here, I say, is a fresh mystery in the history of His humiliation, and the thought of it will cast a new and solemn light on the chapters we shall read during the week. I have said that, after His incarnation, man's nature was as much and as truly Christ's as His Divine attributes; St. Paul even speaks of God 'purchasing us with His own blood,' and of the 'Lord of glory' being 'killed,'[1] – expressions which, more than any other, show how absolutely and simply He had put on Him the nature of man. As the soul acts through the body as its instrument, – in a more perfect way, but as intimately, did the Eternal Word of God act through the manhood which He had taken. When He spoke, it was literally God speaking; when He suffered, it was God suffering. Not that the Divine Nature itself could suffer, any more than our soul can see or hear; but, as the soul sees and hears through the organs of the body, so God the Son suffered in that human nature which He had taken to Himself and made His own. And in that nature He did truly suffer; as truly as He framed the worlds through His Almighty power, so through His human nature did He suffer; for when He came on earth, His manhood became as truly and personally His, as His Almighty power had been from everlasting.

The Incarnate Son, A Sufferer and Sacrifice   PPS VI p. 72–3.   1 April, 1836

---

1   Acts 20, 28; 1 Cor 2, 8

The Mass of Easter Night

Rom 6, 3–11; Luke 24, 1–12

'Why look among the dead?'

Such is the triumphant question with which the Holy Angels put to flight the sadness of the women on the morning of Christ's resurrection. 'O ye of little faith,' less faith than love, more dutiful than understanding, why come ye to anoint His Body on the third day? Why seek ye the Living Saviour in the tomb? The time of sorrow is run out; victory has come, according to His Word, and ye recollect it not. 'He is not here, but is risen!'

These were deeds done and words spoken eighteen hundred years since; so long ago, that in the world's thought they are as though they never had been; yet they hold good to this day. Christ is to us now, just what He was in all His glorious Attributes on the morning of the Resurrection; and we are blessed in knowing it, even more than the women to whom the Angels spoke, according to His own assurance, 'Blessed are they that have not seen, and yet have believed.'[1]

Easter Day. Christ, a Quickening Spirit   PPS II p. 139.   3 April, 1831

Easter Sunday Masses — as for Year A

---

1   John 20, 29

Second Sunday of Easter

Acts 5, 12–16; Rev 1, 9–13. 17–19; John 20, 19–31

'Blessed are they that have not seen'

Now under these circumstances it seemed reasonable that our Lord should give them the testimony of sight, touch, etc., for, unless some one saw Him again, how were the apostles, how was the world to know it.

But a deeper lesson. Sight could not be given to all, because our Lord was going to heaven, and those who did not see must believe on the witness of others. Now the Gospel was to last to the end of the world. Therefore He in His love determined that one of the apostles should be away and not see Him.

This was Thomas, who, being in the state of confusion which they all were in before they saw Him, persisted in that unbelief which at first they all had. When the women testified, the apostles would not believe. When the apostles testified, Thomas would not believe.

We all know what happened. Our Lord graciously granted, etc., but He said: 'Blessed are they that have not seen and have believed.'

This is one lesson Our Lord speaks to us. Thomas thought it hard he had not the evidence the rest had. *He was not content with what was sufficient.* This *the great lesson.* Doubtless sight is more than the witness of other men.

Faith   SN p. 201–2 24 April, 1870 (Low Sunday) PPS VII p. 201–2.
10 May, 1840

Third Sunday of Easter

Acts 5, 27–32. 40–41; Rev 5, 11–14; John 21, 1–19

He calls us again and again

... we are told by St. Luke that this was His gracious employment, when He visited the Apostles from time to time, during the forty days which intervened between Easter Day and the day of His Ascension. 'He showed Himself alive to the Apostles,' says the Evangelist, 'after His passion by many proofs, for forty days appearing to them and speaking of the kingdom of God.'[1] And accordingly, when at length He had ascended on high, and had sent down 'the promise of His Father,' the Holy Ghost, upon His Apostles, they forthwith entered upon their high duties, and brought that kingdom or Church into shape, and supplied it with members, and enlarged it, and carried it into all lands. As to St. Peter, he acted as the head of the Church, according to the previous words of Christ; and, still according to his Lord's supreme will, he at length placed himself in the See of Rome, where he was martyred.

The Pope and the Revolution   OS p. 284.   7 October, 1866

---

1   Acts 1, 3

For in truth we are not called once only, but many times; all through our life Christ is calling us. He called us first in Baptism; but afterwards also; whether we obey His voice or not, He graciously calls us still. If we fall from our Baptism, He calls us to repent; if we are striving to fulfil our calling, He calls us on from grace to grace, and from holiness to holiness, while life is given us. Abraham was called from his home, Peter from his nets, Matthew from his office, Elisha from his farm, Nathanael from his retreat; we are all in course of calling, on and on, from one thing to another, having no resting-place, but mounting towards our eternal rest, and obeying one command only to have another put upon us. He calls us again and again, in order to justify us again and again, − and again and again, and more and more, to sanctify and glorify us.

It were well if we understood this; but we are slow to master the great truth, that Christ is, as it were walking among us, and by His hand, or eye, or voice, bidding us follow Him. We do not understand that His call is a thing which takes place now. We think it took place in the Apostles' days; but we do not believe in it, we do not look out for it in our own case. We have not eyes to see the Lord; far different from the beloved Apostle, who knew Christ even when the rest of the disciples knew Him not. When He stood on the shore after His resurrection, and bade them cast the net into the sea, 'that disciple whom Jesus loved saith unto Peter, It is the Lord.'

Now what I mean is this : that they who are living religiously, have from time to time truths they did not know before, or had not need to consider, brought before them forcibly; truths which involve duties, which are in fact precepts, and claim obedience. In this and such-like ways Christ calls us now. there is nothing miraculous or extraordinary in His dealings with us. He works through our natural faculties and circumstances of life.

Divine Calls PPS VIII p. 23−4. October, 1839

Fourth Sunday of Easter

Acts 13, 14. 43–52; Rev 7, 9. 14–17; John 10, 27–30

'The Father and I are One'

He who spoke was one really existing Person, and He, that one Living and Almighty Son, both God and man, was the brightness of God's glory and His Power, and wrought what His Father willed, and was in the Father and the Father in Him, not only in heaven but on earth. In heaven He was this, and did this, as God; and on earth He was this, and did this, in that manhood which He assumed, but whether in heaven, or on earth, still as the Son. It was therefore true of Him *altogether*, when He spoke, that He was not alone, nor spoke or wrought of Himself, but where He was, there was the Father, and whoso had seen Him had seen the Father, whether we think of Him as God or as man.

Again, we read in Scripture of His being sent by the Father, addressing the Father, interceding to Him for His disciples, and declaring to them that His Father is greater than He; in what sense says and does He all this? Some will be apt to say that He speaks only in His human nature; words which are perplexing to the mind that tries really to contemplate Him as Scripture describes Him, as if He were speaking only under a representation, and not in His Person. No; it is truer to say that He, that One All-gracious Son of God, who had been with the Father from the beginning, equal in all divine perfections and one in substance, but subordinate as being the Son, – as He had ever been His word, and Wisdom, and counsel, and Will, and Power in Heaven, – so after His incarnation, and upon the earth, still spoke and acted after, yet with, the Father as before, though in a new nature, which He had put on, and in humiliation.

This, then, is the second point of doctrine which I had to mention, that our Lord was not only God, but the Son of God. We know more than that God took on Him our flesh; though all is mysterious, we have a point of knowledge further and more distinct, viz. that it was neither the Father nor the Holy Ghost, but the Son of the Father, God the Son, God from God, and Light from Light, who came down upon earth, and who thus, though graciously taking on Him a new nature, remained in Person as He had been from everlasting, the *Son* of the Father, and spoke and acted towards the Father as a Son.

Christ, the Son of God made Man   PPS VI p. 59–61.   26 April, 1836

Fifth Sunday of Easter

Acts 14, 21–27; Rev 21, 1–5; John 13, 31–35

'Love one another ...'

Love, and love only, is the fulfilling of the Law, and they only are in God's favour in whom the righteousness of the Law is fulfilled. This we know full well; yet, alas! at the same time, we cannot deny that whatever good thing we have to show, whether activity, or patience, or faith, or fruitfulness in good works, love to God and man is not ours, or, at least, in very scanty measure; not at all proportionately to our apparent attainments. Now, to enlarge upon this.

In the first place, love clearly does not consist merely in great sacrifices. We can take no comfort to ourselves that we are God's own, merely on the ground of great deeds or great sufferings. The greatest sacrifices without love would be nothing worth, and that they are great does not necessarily prove they are done with love. St. Paul emphatically assures us that his acceptance with God did not stand in any of those high endowments, which strike us in him at first sight, and which, did we actually see him, doubtless would so much draw us to him. One of his highest gifts, for instance, was his spiritual knowledge. He shared, and felt the sinfulness and infirmities of human nature; he had a deep insight into the glories of God's grace, such as no natural man can have. He had an awful sense of the realities of heaven, and of the mysteries revealed. He could have answered ten thousand questions on theological subjects, on all those points about which the Church has disputed since his time, and which we now long to ask him.

Such was this great servant of Christ and Teacher of the Gentiles; yet he says, 'Though I speak with the tongues of men and of Angels, though I have the gift of prophecy, and understand all mysteries, and all knowledge, and have not charity, I am become as sounding brass, or a tinkling cymbal ... I am nothing.'[1] Spiritual discernment, an insight into the Gospel covenant, is no evidence of love.

Love, the One Thing needful PPS V p. 328–9. 10 February, 1839

---

1   I Cor 13, 1

Sixth Sunday of Easter

Acts 15, 1–2. 22–29; Rev 21, 10–14. 22–23; John 14, 23–29

'The Holy Spirit will teach you all things'

And this is one main reason, it would seem, why the Epistles are vouchsafed to us; not so much to increase the Revelation, as to serve as a comment upon it, as taught by our Lord; to bring out and fix His sacred sense, lest we should by any means miss it. That this was the office of the Apostles, and not that of preaching a new and additional revelation, is surely implied by our Lord when He promises them the gift of the Holy Ghost. For instance: 'These things have I spoken unto you,' He says, 'being yet present with you; but the Comforter, which is the Holy Ghost, whom the Father will send in My name, He shall teach you all things, and *bring all things to your remembrance, whatsoever I have said unto you.*' Again, after telling them they could not bear as yet to be told the whole Truth, and that the Holy Spirit would teach it them (words, which do not imply that He had not Himself uttered it, only that He had not conveyed it home to their minds). He proceeds: 'He shall not speak of Himself, but *whatsoever He shall hear, that shall He speak*; and He will show you things to come. He shall *glorify Me*; for *He shall take of Mine, and shall show it unto you.*' Now whatever else these words mean, they seem to imply what the former passage expresses literally, that the Comforter would use and explain Christ's own teaching; not begin anew, but merely develop it. That some deep and heavenly mystery is implied in the words, 'whatsoever He shall hear, that shall He speak,' I doubt not; yet it seems to relate also to what took place on earth. It is part of the condescension of the Persons of the Ever-blessed Trinity, that They vouchsafe to allow the adorable mysteries of heaven to be adumbrated in some inscrutable way on earth. The Eternal Son was subjected to a generation in time; He received the Spirit in time; and the Spirit proceeded from the Father to Him, and them from Both, in time. The texts which speak of what took place in eternity, are also fulfilled in the economy of redemption.[1] And in like manner, I say, whatever else is meant by the words in question, this is meant also, that the Holy Ghost, as is expressly said in the corresponding passage, would bring Christ's words to their remembrance. The office of the Holy Ghost, then, lay in 'glorifying' Christ; in opening the minds of the Apostles for their better remembering, understanding, and preaching of all that was their Lord's, of His person, His mission, His

works, His trials, His sufferings, and among the rest, His words, −
in exalting Him as the Prophet of the Church, as well as her Priest and
King. In one of the clauses it is added, 'He will show you things to
come,' and this will be found to complete the description of the
inspiration which the Apostles received; viz., understanding in our
Lord's words, and the gift of prophecy. Their writings are actually
made up of these two, prophecy and doctrine.

On Scripture as the Record of Our Lord's Teaching   VM I p. 303−4

1   Ps 2, 7

The Ascension of the Lord

Acts 1, 1–11; Eph 1, 17–23; Luke 24, 46–53

'. . . Until you are clothed with power from on high'

'He led them out as far as to Bethany, and He lifted up His hands and blessed them. And it came to pass, while He blessed them, He was parted from them and carried up into heaven.' Surely all His history, all His dealings with them, came before them, gathered up in that moment. Then, as they gazed upon that dread Divine countenance and that heavenly form, every thought and feeling which they ever had had about Him came upon them at once. He had gone through His work; theirs was to come, their work and their sufferings. He was leaving them just at the most critical time.

Yet so it was determined; privileges they were to have, but not the same; and their thoughts henceforth were to be of another kind than heretofore. It was in vain wishing back what was past and over. They were but told, as they gazed, 'This same Jesus, which is taken up from you into heaven, shall so come in like manner as ye have seen Him go into heaven.'

Such are some of the feelings which the Apostles may have experienced on our Lord's ascension; but these are after all but human and ordinary, and of a kind which all of us can enter into; but other than these were sovereign with them at that solemn time, for upon the glorious Ascension of their Lord, 'they worshipped Him,' says the text, 'and returned to Jerusalem with *great joy*, and were continually in the Temple praising and blessing God.'[1]

Warfare the condition of Victory   PPS VI p. 224–5.   24 May, 1838

---

1   Luke 24, 52–53

Thus we are told concerning mankind, that 'in Him we live, and move, and have our being.'[1] And He who lives in all creatures on earth in order to their mortal life, lives in Christians in a more divine way in order to their life immortal; and as we do not know how the creation exists and lives in Him as a Creator, and use words about it beyond our comprehension, so much more (were not comparison out of the question) are we ignorant of the mode or nature of that life of God in the soul, which is the wellspring of the Christian's sanctity, and the seed of everlasting happiness. If this notion of the literal indwelling of God within us, whether in the way of nature or of grace, be decried as a sort of mysticism, I ask in reply whether it is not a necessary truth that He is with and in us, if He is everywhere? And if He is everywhere and dwells in all, there is no antecedent objection against taking Scripture literally, no difficulty in supposing that the truth is as Scripture says, — that as He dwells in us in one mode in the way of nature, so He is in us in another in the way of grace; that His infinite and incomprehensible Essence, which once existed by and in itself alone, and then at the creation so far communicated itself to His works as to sustain what He had brought into existence, and that according to the different measures of life necessary for their respective perfection, may in the Christian Church manifest itself in act and virtue in the hearts of Christians, as far surpassing what it is in unregenerate man, as its presence in man excels its presence in a brute or a vegetable.

The Gift of Righteousness   Jfc p. 145 (1838)

---

1   Acts 17, 28

Seventh Sunday of Easter

Acts 7, 55–60; Rev 22, 12–14. 16–17. 20; John 17, 20–26

'. . . May they be one'

What is told us in the New Testament is to the same purpose. For instance; consider the very precept of Christ, which binds us together in one body, and observe the reason it gives for doing so. 'A new commandment I give unto you, that ye love one another; as I have loved you, that ye also love one another; *by this shall all men know* that ye are My disciples, if ye have love one to another.' You see it was to be a sign to the world, not to the Church herself. Still more clearly is this implied in our Lord's intercessory prayer: 'As Thou, Father, art in Me, and I in Thee, that they also may be one in Us, that the *world may believe* that Thou hast sent Me.' You see, unity was for the sake of the world; He repeats it: 'I in them, and Thou in Me, that they may be perfect in one, and *that the world may know* that Thou hast sent Me, and hast loved them, as Thou hast loved Me.' The visibility of the Church was rather for her proclaiming the truth, than for her dispensing grace. Again: 'Ye are the *light of the world*; a city that is set on a hill cannot be hid . . . Let your light *so shine before men*, that they may see your good works, and *glorify your Father* which is in heaven.' And we see our Saviour's precepts and prayers actually fulfilled in the first days of His Church: 'And they continued steadfastly in the Apostles' doctrine and fellowship, and in breaking of bread, and in prayers'; and what was the consequence? *'and fear came upon every soul.'* But let us proceed with the passage: 'They continuing daily with one accord in the temple, and breaking bread from house to house, did eat their meat with gladness and singleness of heart, praising God'; – and what followed? – 'and *having favour with all the people.'* And again, observe the result of this unanimity: 'And the Lord *added to the Church* daily such as should be saved.'[1]

Outward and Inward Notes of the Church   SD p. 330–1.   5 December, 1841

1   John 13, 34. 35; 17, 21. 23; Matt 5, 14. 16; Acts 2, 42. 43. 46. 47.

Every one who desires unity, who prays for it, who endeavours to further it, who witnesses for it, who behaves Christianly towards the members of Churches alienated from us, who is at amity with them, (saving his duty to his own communion and to the truth itself), who tries to edify them, while he edifies himself and his own people, may surely be considered, as far as he himself is concerned, as breaking down the middle wall of division, and renewing the ancient bonds of unity and concord by the power of charity. Charity can do all things for us; charity is at once a spirit of zeal and of peace; by charity we shall faithfully protest against what our private judgment warrants us in condemning in others; and by charity we have it in our own hands, let all men oppose us, to restore in our own circle the intercommunion of the Churches.

Private Judgment   Ess II p. 174. July 1841
(an article in the *British Critic*)

Pentecost – Readings as for Year A

Pentecost Sunday

Acts 2, 1–11; Rom 8, 8–17; John 14, 15–16. 23–26

'. . . And we shall come to him and make our home with him'

It was the great promise of the Gospel, that the Lord of all, who had hitherto manifested Himself externally to His servants, should take up His abode in their hearts. This, as you must recollect, is frequently the language of the Prophets; and it was the language of our Saviour when He came on earth: 'I will love him,' He says, speaking of those who love and obey Him, 'and will manifest Myself to him . . . We will come unto him, and make our abode with him.'[1] Though He had come in our flesh, so as to be seen and handled, even this was not enough. Still He was external and separate; but after His ascension He descended again by and in His Spirit, and then at length the promise was fulfilled.

There must indeed be a union between all creatures and their Almighty Creator even for their very existence; for it is said, 'In Him we live, and move, and have our being'; and in one of the Psalms, 'When Thou lettest Thy breath go forth, they shall be made.'[2] But far higher, more intimate, and more sacred is the indwelling of God in the hearts of His elect people; – so intimate, that compared with it, He may well be said not to inhabit other men at all; His presence being specified as the characteristic privilege of His own redeemed servants.

From the day of Pentecost, to the present time, it has been their privilege, according to the promise, 'I will pray the Father, and He shall give you another Comforter, that He may abide with you *for ever*,' – for ever; not like the Son of man, who having finished His gracious work went away. Then it is added, 'even the *Spirit of Truth*'; that is, He who came for ever, came as a Spirit, and, so coming, did for His own that which the visible flesh and blood of the Son of man, from its very nature, could not do, viz., He came into the souls of all who believe, and taking possession of them, He, being One, knit them all together into one. Christ, by coming in the flesh, provided an external or apparent unity, such as had been under the Law. He formed His Apostles into a visible society; but when He came again in the Person of His Spirit, He made them all in a real sense one, not in name only. For they were no longer arranged merely in the form of unity, as the limbs of the dead may be, but they were parts and organs of one unseen power; they really depended upon, and were offshoots of that which was One; their separate persons were taken into a mysterious union with things unseen, were grafted upon and assimilated to the spiritual body of Christ, which is One, even by the Holy Ghost, in whom Christ has come again to us.

The Communion of Saints   PPS IV p. 168–9.   14 May, 1837

1   John 14, 21. 23
2   Ps 104, 30 (*B.C.P.*)

The Most Holy Trinity

Prov 8, 22–31; Rom 5, 1–5; John 16, 12–15

The Holy Spirit in the Church

Hence it appears that the Gospels are the great instruments (under God's blessing) of fixing and instructing our minds in a religious course, the Epistles being rather comments on them than intended to supersede them, as is sometimes maintained. Surely it argues a temper of mind but partially moulded to the worship and love of Christ, to make this distinction between His teaching and that of His Apostles, when the very promised office of the Comforter in His absence was, not to make a new revelation, but expressly 'to bring all things to their remembrance' which '*He* had said to them'; *not* to 'speak of Himself,' but 'to receive of Christ's, and show it unto them.' The Holy Spirit came 'to glorify Christ,' to declare openly to all the world that *He* had come on earth, suffered, and died, who was also the Creator and Governor of the world, the Saviour, the final Judge of men. It is the Incarnation of the Son of God rather than any doctrine drawn from a partial view of Scripture (however true and momentous it may be) which is the article of a standing or a falling Church. 'Every spirit that confesseth not that Jesus Christ is come *in the flesh*, is not of God; ... this is that spirit of anti-Christ'; for, not to mention other more direct considerations, it reverses, as far as in it lies, all that the revealed character of Christ has done for our faith and virtue. And hence the Apostles' speeches in the book of Acts and the primitive Creeds insist almost exclusively upon the history, not the doctrines, of Christianity; it being designed that, by means of our Lord's Economy, the great doctrines of theology should be taught, the facts of that Economy giving its peculiarity and force to the Revelation.

The Influence of Natural and Revealed Religion Respectively   US p. 34–5
13 April, 1830

The Body and Blood of Christ

Gen 14, 18−20; 1 Cor 11, 23−26; Luke 9, 11−17

The feeding of the Five thousand and the Holy Eucharist

If the marvellousness of the miracle of the loaves is no real objection to its truth, neither is the marvellousness of the Eucharistic presence any real difficulty in our believing that gift.

And as if still more closely to connect this Holy Sacrament with the miracle of the Loaves, and to make the latter interpret the former, our Lord, as I have observed, wrought the miracle of the loaves by means of the same outward acts, which He observed in the mystery of His Supper, and which His Apostles have carefully recorded as the appointed means of consecrating it. St. John says, 'He *took* the loaves, and when *He had given thanks*, He *distributed* to the disciples.' Compare this with St. Luke's account of the institution of the Lord's Supper. 'He *took* bread, and *gave thanks*, and brake it, and *gave* unto them.' ...

One cannot doubt, then, that the taking bread, blessing or giving thanks, and breaking is a necessary form in the Lord's Supper, since it is so much insisted on in these narratives; and it evidently betokens something extraordinary, − else why *should* it be insisted on? − and what that is, the miracle of the Loaves tells us. For there the same form is observed, and there it was Christ's outward instrument in working a great 'work of God.' The feeding then of the multitude with the loaves, interprets the Lord's Supper; and as the one is a supernatural work, so is the other also.

The Eucharistic Presence   PPS VI p. 146−8.   13 May, 1838

The Sacred Heart of Jesus

Ezek 34, 11–16; Rom 5, 5–11; Luke 15, 3–7

Christ's Love for Us

We too, in our way, are each of us one, though we are two – soul and body – and the body has parts; (nevertheless)[1] each of us is *one*. This is what is meant by speaking of our Lord's (oneness) as we speak of our own.

And though each of us is thus composite, we can love each other as one, though of so many parts. And in like manner, though our Lord is God and man, with a soul (and body), we can contemplate Him as one, and worship, love Him as one.

Further, if I said I loved the face, or the smile, or liked to take the hand of my father or mother, it would be because I loved them. And so, when I speak of the separate portions of our Lord's human frame, I really am worshipping Him. So in the Blessed Sacrament we do not conceive of His Body and Blood as separate from Him.

Devotions at various times (and ages) – the Wounds, the Blood, the Face – and in like manner the Heart. *We worship (each) as Him*, as that One Person who is God and man; we worship (*Him*) by the memento, the pledge of His Heart.

Why? The Heart a *symbol* – so the Wounds and the Blood. (In contrast with these) a symbol is sometimes that which (only) expresses and reminds – thus water, oil, wine, bread.

What is the Heart the symbol of? – of His love, His affection for us, so that He suffered for us – the agony in the garden.

Moreover, of His love in the Holy Eucharist.

The Heart was the seat, first, of His love for us; secondly, of His many griefs and sorrows.

The Sacred Heart   SN p. 258–9.   6 June, 1875

---

1   alternative readings in the manuscript

O Sacred Heart of Jesus, I adore Thee in the oneness of the Personality of the Second Person of the Holy Trinity. Whatever belongs to the Person of Jesus, belongs therefore to God, and is to be worshipped with that one and the same worship which we pay to Jesus. He did not take on Him His human nature, as something distinct and separate from Himself, but as simply, absolutely, eternally His, so as to be included by us in the very thought of Him. I worship Thee, O Heart of Jesus, as being Jesus Himself, as being that Eternal Word in human nature which He took wholly and lives in wholly, and therefore in Thee. Thou art the Heart of the Most High made man. In worshipping Thee, I worship my Incarnate God, Emmanuel.

MD p. 571

Second Sunday of the Year

Isa 62, 1–5; 1 Cor 12, 4–11; John 2, 1–11

The Marriage Feast at Cana

Thus in the Gospel for the First Sunday, He manifests His glory in the temple at the age of twelve years, sitting among the doctors, and astonishing them with His wisdom. In the Gospel for the Second Sunday He manifests His glory at the wedding feast, when He turned the water into wine, a miracle not of necessity or urgency, but especially an august and bountiful act – the act of a King, who out of His abundance gave a gift to His own, therewith to make merry with their friends.

   Such is the series of manifestations which the Sundays after the Epiphany bring before us. When He is with the doctors in the temple, He is manifested as a prophet – in turning the water into wine, as a priest.

The Season of Epiphany   PPS VII p. 76–7.   17 January, 1841

Nay, may we not say that our Lord Himself had commenced His ministry, that is, bade farewell to His earthly home, at a feast? for it was at the marriage entertainment at Cana of Galilee that He did His first miracle, and manifested forth His glory. He was in the house of friends, He was surrounded by intimates and followers, and He took a familiar interest in the exigences of the feast. He supplied a principal want which was interfering with their festivity. It was His contribution to it. By supplying it miraculously He showed that He was beginning a new life, the life of a Messenger from God, and that that feast was the last scene of the old life. And, moreover, He made use of one remarkable expression, which seems to imply that this change of condition really was in His thoughts, if we may dare so to speak of them, or at all to interpret them. For when His Mother said unto Him, 'They have no wine,' He answered, 'What have I to do with thee?'

Our Lord's Last Supper and His First   SD p. 31–2.   26 February, 1843

Third Sunday of the Year

Neh 8, 2–6. 8–10; 1 Cor 12, 12–30; Luke 1, 1–4. 4. 14–21

The Coming of our Redeemer

Such is the world: but Christ came to make a new world. He came into the world to regenerate it in Himself, to make a new beginning, to be the beginning of the creation of God, to gather together in one, and recapitulate all things in Himself. The rays of His glory were scattered through the world; one state of life had some of them, another others. The world was like some fair mirror, broken in pieces, and giving back no one uniform image of its Maker. But He came to combine what was dissipated, to recast what was shattered in Himself. He began all excellence, and of His fulness have all we received.

The Three Offices of Christ   SD p. 61.   25 December, 1840

But the Almighty Lover of souls looked once again; and He saw in that poor, forlorn, and ruined nature, which He had in the beginning filled with grace and light, He saw in it, not what merited His favour, not what would adequately respond to His influences, not what was a necessary instrument of His purposes, but what would illustrate and preach abroad His grace, if He took pity on it. He saw in it, a natural nobleness, a simplicity, a frankness of character, a love of truth, a zeal for justice, an indignation at wrong, an admiration of purity, a reverence for law, a keen appreciation of the beautifulness and majesty of order, nay, further, a tenderness and an affectionateness of heart, which He knew would become the glorious instruments of His high will, when illuminated and vivified by His supernatural gifts. And so He who, did it so please Him, could raise up children to Abraham out of the very stones of the earth, nevertheless determined in this instance in His free mercy to unite what was beautiful in nature with what was radiant in grace; and, as if those poor Anglo-Saxons had been too fair to be heathen, therefore did He rescue them from the devil's service and the devil's doom, and bring them into the house of His holiness and the mountain of His rest.

Christ upon the Waters   OS p. 126–7.   27 October, 1850

Fourth Sunday of the Year

Jer 1, 4–5. 17–19; 1 Cor 12, 31–13, 13; Luke 4, 21–30

Lack of Faith in Christ

Let us, in like manner, feel certain, as well we may, that however great are the disorders of this present age, and though the unbelieving seek and find not, yet that to the humble and lowly, the earnest-minded and pure in heart, the Lord God of Elijah still reveals Himself. The Presence of Christ is still among us, in spite of our many sins and the sins of our people. 'The spirit and power of Elias' should now especially be with us, because the notes of his day are among us. What is the token of his coming but a backsliding age? what are the notes of that Man of God, but dimness and confusion, the threatenings of evil, the scattering of the faithful, and the defection of the powerful?' In the way of Thy judgments, O Lord, have we waited for Thee; the desire of our soul is to Thy Name, and to the remembrance of Thee. With my soul have I desired Thee in the night, yea with my spirit within me will I seek Thee early.' 'Although the fig-tree shall not blossom, neither shall fruit be in the vines; the labour of the olive shall fail, and the fields shall yield no meat; the flock shall be cut off from the fold, and there shall be no herd in the stalls; yet I will rejoice in the Lord, I will joy in the God of my salvation.'[1]

What want we then but faith in our church? with faith we can do everything; without faith we can do nothing. If we have a secret misgiving about her, all is lost; we lose our nerve, our powers, our position, our hope. A cold despondency and sickness of mind, a niggardness and peevishness of spirit, a cowardice and a sluggishness, envelope us, penetrate us, stifle us. Let it not be so with us; let us be of good heart; let us accept her as God's gift and our portion; let us imitate him, who, when he was 'by the bank of Jordan, ... took the mantle of Elijah, that fell from him, and smote the waters, and said, Where is the Lord God of Elijah?'[2] She is like the mantle of Elijah, a relic from Him who is gone up on high.

Elijah the Prophet of the Latter Days   SD p. 379–80.   12 December, 1841

---

1   Isa. 26, 8. 9. Hab. 3, 17, 18
2   2 Kgs. 2, 13, 14

Fifth Sunday of the Year

Isa 6, 1 – 8; 1 Cor 15, 1 – 11; Luke 5, 1 – 11

In the Presence of our Lord and God

Let us then take this view of religious service; it is 'going out to meet the Bridegroom,' who, if not seen 'in His beauty,' will appear in consuming fire. Besides its other momentous reasons, it is a preparation for an awful event, which shall one day be. What it would be to meet Christ at once without preparation, we may learn from what happened even to the Apostles when His glory was suddenly manifested to them. St. Peter said, 'Depart from me, for I am a sinful man, O Lord.' And St. John, 'when he saw Him, fell at His feet as dead.'[1]

This being the case, it is certainly most merciful in God to vouchsafe to us the means of preparation, and such means as He has actually appointed. When Moses came down from the Mount, and the people were dazzled at his countenance, he put a veil over it. That veil is so far removed in the Gospel, that we are in a state of preparation for its being altogether removed. We are with Moses in the Mount so far, that we have a sight of God; we are with the people beneath it so far, that Christ does not visibly show Himself. He has put a veil on, and He sits among us silently and secretly. When we approach Him, we know it only by faith; and when He manifests Himself to us, it is without our being able to realize to ourselves that manifestation.

Such then is the spirit in which we should come to all His ordinances, considering them as anticipations and first-fruits of that sight of Him which one day must be. When we kneel down in prayer in private, let us think to ourselves, Thus shall I one day kneel down before His very footstool, in this flesh and this blood of mine; and He will be seated over against me, in flesh and blood also, though divine. I come, with the thought of that awful hour before me, I come to confess my sin to Him now, that He may pardon it then, and I say, 'O Lord, Holy God, Holy and Strong, Holy and Immortal, in the hour of death and in the day of Judgment, deliver us, O Lord!'[2]

Worship, a Preparation for Christ's Coming   PPS V p. 8 – 9.   2 December, 1838

---

1   Luke 5, 8 Rev.1, 17.
2   based on the Good Friday *Reproaches*.

Sixth Sunday of the Year

Jer 17, 5–8; 1 Cor 15, 12. 16–20; Luke 6, 17. 20–26

'Happy are you who are poor'

And now in turn, what did the second and greater Prophet of the Church declare, when He was set upon the Mount, with the people around Him, and published His covenant of grace. 'He opened His mouth and said, Blessed are the poor in spirit, for theirs is the kingdom of heaven. Blessed are they that mourn, for they shall be comforted. Blessed are the meek ... Blessed are they which do hunger and thirst after righteousness ... Blessed are the merciful ... Blessed are the pure in heart ... Blessed are the peacemakers.' ...

At another time He spoke thus: 'Sell that ye have, and give alms.' 'If thou wilt be perfect, go and sell that thou hast, and give to the poor.' 'It is easier for a camel to go through the eye of a needle, than for a rich man to enter into the kingdom of God.' 'Whosoever will be chief among you, let him be your servant.' 'If any man will come after Me, let him deny himself, and take up his cross, and follow Me.' And, in a word, the doctrine of the Gospel, and the principle of it, is thus briefly stated by the Apostle, in the words of the Wise Man. 'Whom the Lord loveth He chasteneth, and scourgeth every son whom He receiveth. If ye endure chastening. God dealeth with you as with sons ... If ye be without chastisement, *whereof all are partakers*, then are ye bastards, and not sons.'[1] Can words speak it plainer, that, as certainly as temporal prosperity is the gift of the Law, so also are hardship and distress the gift of the Gospel?

Take up thy portion, then, Christian soul, and weigh it well, and learn to love it. Thou wilt find, if thou art Christ's, in spite of what the world fancies, that after all, even at this day, endurance, in a special sense, *is* the lot of those who offer themselves to be servants of the King of sorrows. There is an inward world, which none see but those who belong to it; and though the outside robe be many-coloured, like Joseph's coat, inside it is lined with camel's hair, or sackcloth, fitting those who desire to be one with Him who fared hardly in the wilderness, in the mountain, and on the sea.

Endurance. The Christian's Portion   PPS V p. 293. 294–5.   3 March, 1839

1   Luke 12, 33; Matt 19, 21. 24; 20, 27; 26, 24; Heb 12, 6–8.

Seventh Sunday of the Year

1 Sam 26, 2. 7–9. 12–13. 22–23; 11 Cor 15, 45–49; Luke 6,
27–38

Loving our Enemies

Of course it is absolutely sinful to have any private enmities. Not
the bitterest personal assaults upon us should induce us to retaliate.
We must do good for evil, 'love those who hate, bless those who
curse us, and pray for those who despitefully use us.' It is only
when it is impossible at once to be kind to them, and give glory to
God, that we may cease to act kindly towards them. When David
speaks of hating God's enemies, it was under circumstances when
keeping friends with them would have been a desertion of the Truth.
St. James says, 'Know ye not that the friendship of the world is
enmity with God?'[1] and so, on the other hand, devotion to God's
cause is enmity with the world. But no personal feeling must intrude
itself in any case. We hate sinners, by putting them out of our sight,
as if they were not, by annihilating them, in our affections. And
this we must do, even in the case of our friends and relations, if
God requires it. But in no case are we to allow ourselves in resentment
or malice.

   Next, it is quite compatible with the most earnest zeal, to offer kind
offices to God's enemies when in distress. I do not say that a denial of
these offices may not be a duty ordinarily; for it is our duty, as St.
John tells us in his second Epistle, not even to receive them into our
houses. But the case is very different where men are brought into
extremity. God 'maketh His sun to rise on the evil and on the good,
and sendeth rain on the just and on the unjust.'[2] We must go and do
likewise, imitating the good Samaritan; and as he thought nothing of
difference of nations when a Jew was in distress, in like manner we
must not take account of wilful heresy, or profaneness, in such
circumstances.

   And, further, the Christian keeps aloof from sinners in order to do
them good. He does so in the truest and most enlarged charity. It is a
narrow and weak feeling to please a man here, and to endanger his
soul. A true friend is he who speaks out, and, when a man sins, shows
his friend's sin, is 'partaker of his evil deeds.'[3] The Psalmist speaks
in this spirit, when, after praying to God 'to persecute' the ungodly

'with His tempest,' he adds, 'fill their faces with shame, that they may seek Thy name, O Lord.'[4]

A Pattern to Christians   PPS III p. 184–6.   8 June, 1834

1   Jas 4, 4
2   Matt 5, 45
3   2 John 11
4   Ps 83, 16, (*B.C.P.*)

Eighth Sunday of the Year

Sir 27, 4–7; 1 Cor 15, 54–58; Luke 6, 39–45

'Let love be unhypocritical'

An honest, unaffected desire of doing right is the test of God's true servants. On the other hand, a double mind, a pursuing other ends besides the truth, and in consequence an inconsistency in conduct, and a half-consciousness (to say the least) of inconsistency, and a feeling of the necessity of defending oneself, and to God, and to the world; in a word, hypocrisy; these are the signs of the merely professed Christian. Now I am going to give some instances of this distinction, in Scripture and in fact.

For instance. The two great Christian graces are faith and love. Now, how are these characterised in Scripture? – By their being honest or single-minded. Thus St. Paul, in one place, speaks of 'the end of the commandment being love'; what love? – 'love *out of a pure heart*,' he proceeds, 'and of a *good conscience*'; and still further, 'and of faith,' – what kind of faith? – 'faith *unfeigned*'; or, as it may be more literally translated, 'unhypocritical faith;' for so the word means in Greek. Again, elsewhere he speaks of his 'calling to remembrance the *unfeigned* faith' which dwelt in Timothy, and in his mother and grandmother before him; that is, literally, 'unhypo-critical faith.' Again, he speaks of the Apostles approving themselves as the ministers of God, 'by kindness, by the Holy Ghost, by love *unfeigned*,' or, more literally, 'unhypocritical love.' Again, as to love towards man. 'Let love be *without dissimulation*,' or, more literally, as in the other cases, 'let love be unhypocritical.' In like manner, St. Peter speaks of Christians 'having purified their souls in obeying the truth through the Spirit unto unhypocritical love of the brethren.' And in like manner, St. James speaks of 'the wisdom that is from above, being first *pure* ...' and, presently, 'without partiality, and *without* hypocrisy.'[1] Surely it is very remarkable that three Apostles, writing on different subjects and occasions, should each of them thus speak about whether faith or love as without hypocrisy.

Sincerity and Hypocrisy   PPS V p. 224–5.   16 December, 1838

1   2 Cor 6, 6; Rom 12, 9. 1 Pet 1, 22. Jas 3, 17.

Ninth Sunday of the Year

1 Kgs 8, 41–43; Gal 1, 1–2. 6–10; Luke 7, 1–10

Obedience to the Word of God

Those who surrender themselves to Christ in implicit faith are graciously taken into His service; and, 'as men under authority,' they do great things without knowing it, by the Wisdom of their Divine Master. They act on conscience, perhaps in despondency, and without foresight; but what is obedience in them, has a purpose with God, and they are successful, when they do but mean to be dutiful. But what duplicity does the world think it, to speak of conscience, or honour, or propriety, or delicacy, or to give other tokens of personal motives, when the event seems to show that a calculation of results has been the actuating principle at bottom! It is God who designs, but His servants seem designing; and that the more, should it so happen that they really do themselves catch glimpses of their own position in His providential course. For then what they do from the heart, approves itself to their reason, and they are able to recognize the expedience of obedience.

Wisdom and Innocence   SD p. 305.   19 February, 1843

Tenth Sunday of the Year

1 Kgs 17, 17–24; Gal 1, 11–19; Luke 7, 11–17

The widow's Son raised to life

INTROD. – The Holy Fathers are accustomed to derive a spiritual lesson from the miracle recorded in the gospel of this day. It was a miracle exercised on one, but it was a sort of specimen of what takes place by God's love so often. It was done once, but it images what occurs continually.

This was a young man borne out to his burial, and his mother is weeping over him.

The mother is the Church, who has born him in baptism, when he was born again and became her child.

He has fallen away, and is dead in sin. He is here carried on his way, like Dives, to be buried in hell.

How awfully he is carried forth! Slowly, but sure, as the course of a funeral.

Describe his odiousness – death so fearful, every one shrinks from the sight. Children in the streets turn away. Those only bear it who love the corpse, or have duties towards it. So *with the soul*. How angels must shrink from the dead soul! – the guardian angel bears it. How horrible it looks even (if in)[1] venial sin, much more in mortal!

The mother bears it – the Church does not ex-communicate.

Its bearers are four: (1) pride, (2) sensuality, (3) unbelief, (4) ignorance. We see these from Adam's original sin, and they are in every sinner, though perhaps in a different order in different persons. There are those who go on, through God's mercy, in the right way. But I am speaking of cases of sin.

Now I believe generally pride comes first – obstinacy of children; disobedience; quarrelling; refusing to say prayers; avoiding holy places, etc. Thus the soul being left open to the evil one, he proceeds to assault it with sensuality.

Sensuality. A person does not know when he is proud, but this (sensuality) need not be described, for every one who yields to it knows what it is. God has set a mark upon it, the mark of sting of conscience, because it is so pleasant; whereas pride is unpleasant to the person who exercises it.

Thirdly, unbelief. Pride and sensuality give birth to unbelief. A man begins to doubt and disbelieve.

Fourth, ignorance. At last he does not know right from wrong.

And thus a soul is led out to be buried, to be buried *in hell*. And how many reach that eternal tomb!

Wonderful electing grace of God, choosing one and not another, coming without merit – the Church cannot do it.

We all have received it (this electing grace) without merit. Let us prize it when we have it.

SN p.131–3.   29 August, 1856

1   alternative readings in the manuscript

There is so much alike at first sight in the history of Elijah and Elisha, that it is not surprising if many of us (as I suppose is the case) confuse them one with the other. Yet if we examine the sacred narrative carefully, we shall find that they differ from each other as widely as those children in the market-place, described by our Lord, the figures of Himself and St. John Baptist, who first piped and then mourned. Certainly there are many things which correspond in their respective histories. Both wrought miracles; both withstood kings; both, at God's bidding, visited in mercy the heathen in their neighbourhood; both lived in one age and one country, and apparently with one principal design in God's Providence, viz. that of witnessing against idolatry. Even the same miracles were wrought by the one and the other; both multiplied oil; both raised a dead child: so far they resemble each other.

Elisha a Type of Christ   SD p. 164–5.   14 August, 1836

Eleventh Sunday of the Year

2 Sam 12, 7–10. 13; Gal 2, 16. 19–21; Luke 7, 36–8, 3

In the House of Simon the Pharisee

When sinners truly repent, then, indeed, they are altogether brothers in Christ's kingdom with those who have not in the same sense 'need of repentance'; but that they should repent at all is (alas!) so far from being likely, that when the unexpected event takes place it causes such joy in heaven (from the marvellousness of it) as is not even excited by the ninety and nine just persons who need no such change of mind.[1] Of such changes some instances are given us in the Gospels for the encouragement of all penitents, such as that of the woman, mentioned by St. Luke, who 'loved much.' Christ most graciously went among sinners, if so be He might save them; and we know that even those open sinners, when they knew that they were sinners, were nearer salvation, and in a better state, than the covetous and irreligious Pharisees, who added to their other gross sins, hypocrisy, blindness, a contempt of others, and a haughty and superstitious reliance on the availing virtue of their religious privileges.

Obedience to God the Way to Faith in Christ   PPS VIII p. 209.
31 October, 1830

---

1   Luke 15, 7

Twelfth Sunday of the Year

Zech 12, 10–11. 13, 1; Gal 3, 26–29; Luke 9, 18–24

Proclaiming the Truth to the World

We rejoice, not 'as those who rejoice in the harvest, or as conquerors rejoice when they divide the spoils.' We rejoice surely, but solemnly, religiously, courageously, as the priests of the Lord, when they were carrying into battle 'the ark of the Lord, the God of the whole earth.' We rejoice, as those who love men's souls so well that they would go through much to save them, yet love God more, and find the full reward of all disappointments in Him; as those whose work lies with sinners, but whose portion is with the saints. We love you, O men of this generation, but we fear you not. Understand well and lay it to heart, that we will do the work of God and fulfil our mission, with your consent, if we can get it, but in spite of you, if we cannot. You cannot touch us except in a way of which you do not dream, by the arm of force; nor do we dream of asking for more than that which the Apostle claimed, freedom of speech, 'an open door,' which, through God's grace, will be 'evident,' though there be 'many adversaries.' We do but wish to subdue you by appeals to your reason and to your heart; give us but a fair field and in due time, and we hope to gain our point. I do not say we shall gain it in this generation; I do not say we shall gain it without our own suffering; but we look on to the future, and we do not look at ourselves. As to ourselves, the world has long ago done its worst against us: long ago has it seasoned us for this encounter. In the way of obloquy and ridicule it has exhausted upon us long since all it had to pour, and now it is resourceless. More it cannot say against us than it has said already. We have parted company with it for many years; we have long chosen our portion with the old faith once delivered to the saints, and we have intimately comprehended that a penalty is attached to the profession. No one proclaims the truth to a deceived world, but will be treated himself as a deceiver. We know our place and our fortunes: to give a witness, and to be reviled; to be cast out as evil, and to succeed. Such is the law which the Lord of all has annexed to the promulgation of the truth: its preachers suffer, but its cause prevails. Joyfully have we become a party to this bargain; and as we have resigned ourselves to the price, so we intend, by God's aid, to claim the compensation.

Christ upon the Waters OS p. 159–60. 27 October, 1850. St Chad's, Birmingham

1 Isa 9, 2; Josh 3, 13

Thirteenth Sunday of the Year

1 Kgs 19, 16. 19–21; Gal 5, 1. 13–18; Luke 9, 51–62

Carrying our Cross

Again: consider the following declaration of our Saviour: He first tells us, 'Strait is the gate, and narrow is the way which leadeth to life, and few there be that find it.' And again: 'Strive to enter in, for many, I say unto you, will seek (only seek) to enter in, and shall not be able.' Then He explains to us what this peculiar difficulty of a Christian's life consists in: 'If any man come to Me, and hate not his father, and mother, and wife, and children, and brethren, and sisters, yea, and his own life also, he cannot be My disciple[1].' Now whatever is precisely meant by this (which I will not here stop to inquire), so far is evident, that our Lord enjoins a certain refraining, not merely from sin, but from innocent comforts and enjoyments of this life, or a self-denial in things lawful.

Again, He says, 'If any man will come after Me, let him deny himself, and take up his cross daily, and follow Me.' Here He shows us from His own example what Christian self-denial is. It is taking on us a cross after His pattern, not a mere refraining from sin, for He had no sin, but a giving up what we might lawfully use. This was the peculiar character in which Christ came on earth. It was this spontaneous and exuberant self-denial which brought Him down. He who was one with God, took upon Him our nature, and suffered death – and why? to save us whom He needed not save. Thus He denied Himself, and took up His cross.

The Duty of Self-denial   PPS VII p. 90–1.   28 March, 1830

---

1   Matt 7, 14; Luke 13, 24. 14, 26.

Fourteenth Sunday of the Year

Isa 66, 10–14; Gal 6, 14–18; Luke 10, 1–12. 17–20

... Sent out by Christ into the world

For it is your brethren whom He has appointed, and none else, – sons of Adam, sons of your nature, the same by nature, differing only in grace, – men, like you, exposed to temptations, to the same temptations, to the same warfare within and without; with the same three deadly enemies – the world, the flesh, and the devil; with the same human, the same wayward heart: differing only as the power of God has changed and rules it. So it is; we are not Angels from Heaven that speak to you, but men, whom grace, and grace alone, has made to differ from you.

Men, not Angels, the Priests of the Gospel   Mix p. 45 (Discourse 3) 1849

'Behold, I send you forth as sheep in the midst of wolves';[1] what our Lord addressed to His Apostles is fulfilled to this day in all those who obey Him. They are sprinkled up and down the world; they are separated the one from the other, they are bid quit each other's dear society, and sent afar off to those who are differently minded. Their choice of profession and employment is not their own. Outward circumstances, over which they have no control, determine their line of life; accidents bring them to this place or that place, not knowing whither they go; not knowing the persons to whom they unite themselves, they find, almost blindly, their home and their company. And in this, moreover, differing from the Apostles, and very painfully; that the Apostles knew each other, and could communicate one with another, and could form, nay, were bound to form one body; but now, those honest and true hearts, in which the good seed has profitably fallen, do not even know each other; nay, even when they think they can single out their fellows, yet are they not allowed to form a separate society with them.

The Visible Church an Encouragement to Faith   PPS III pp. 239.
14 September, 1834

1   Matt 10, 16

Fifteenth Sunday of the Year

Deut 30, 10–14; Col 1, 15–20; Luke 10, 25–37

The Good Samaritan

Again: He has made the poor, weak, and afflicted, tokens and instruments of His Presence; and here again, as is plain, the same temptation meets us to neglect or profane it. What He was, such are His chosen followers in this world; and as His obscure and defenceless state led men to insult and ill-treat Him, so the like peculiarities, in the tokens of His presence, lead men to insult Him now. That such are His tokens is plain from many passages of Scripture: for instance, He says of children, 'Whoso shall receive one such little child in My Name, receiveth Me.' Again: He said to Saul, who was persecuting His followers, 'Why persecutest thou Me?' And He forewarns us, that at the Last Day He will say to the righteous, 'I was an hungered, and ye gave Me meat; I was thirsty, and ye gave Me drink; I was a stranger, and ye took Me in; naked, and ye clothed Me; I was sick and ye visited Me; I was in prison, and ye came unto Me.' And He adds, 'Inasmuch as ye have done it unto the least of these My brethren, ye have done it unto Me'[1] He observes the same connexion between Himself and His followers in His words to the wicked. What makes this passage the more awful and apposite, is this, which has been before now remarked,[2] that neither righteous nor wicked *knew* what they had done; even the righteous are represented as unaware that they had approached Christ. They say, 'Lord, *when* saw we Thee an hungered, and fed Thee, or thirsty, and gave Thee drink?' In every age, then, Christ is both in the world, and yet not publicly so more than in the days of His flesh.

Christ Hidden from the World   PPS IV p. 250–1.   25 December, 1837

---

1   Matt. 18, 5. Acts 9, 4. Matt. 25, 35–40
2   *Vide* Pascal's *Pensées*

Sixteenth Sunday of the Year

Gen 18, 1–10; Col 1, 24–28; Luke 10, 38–42

Martha and Mary

Such being the two-fold character of Christian obedience, I observe, secondly, that Mary's portion is the better of the two. Our Lord does not expressly say so, but He clearly implies it: 'Martha, Martha, thou art careful and troubled about many things; but one thing is needful: and Mary hath chosen that good part, which shall not be taken away from her.' If His words be taken literally, they might, indeed, even mean that Martha's heart was not right with Him, which, it is plain from other parts of the history, they do not mean. Therefore, what He intimated surely was, that Martha's portion was full of snares, as being one of worldly labour, but that Mary could not easily go wrong in hers; that we may be busy in a wrong way, we cannot well adore Him except in a right one; that to serve God by prayer and praise continually, when we can do so consistently with other duties, is the pursuit of the 'one thing needful,' and emphatically 'that good part which shall not be taken away from us.'

The Good Part of Mary   PPS III p. 326–7.   October, 1834

Seventeenth Sunday of the Year

Gen 18, 20–32; Col 2, 12–14; Luke 11, 1–13

The Need for Prayer

I now come to the second reason for stated private prayer. Besides its tending to produce in us lasting religious impressions, which I have already enlarged upon, it is also a more direct means of gaining from God an answer to our requests. He has so sanctioned it in the text: − 'Shut thy door, and pray to thy Father which seeth in secret, and He shall reward thee openly.'[1] We do not know *how* it is that prayer receives an answer from God at all. It is strange, indeed, that weak man should have strength to move God; but it is our privilege to know that we *can* do so. The whole system of this world is a history of man's interfering with Divine decrees; and if we have the melancholy power of baffling His good-will, to our own ruin (an awful, an incomprehensible truth!), if, when He designs our eternal salvation, we can yet annul our heavenly election, and accomplish our eternal destruction, much more have we the power to move Him (blessed be His name!) when He, the Searcher of hearts, discerns in us the mind of that Holy Spirit, which 'maketh intercession for the saints according to His will.' And, as He has thus promised an answer to our poor prayers, so it is not more strange that prayers offered up at particular times, and in a particular way, should have especially prevailing power with Him. And the reason of it may be as follows. It is faith that is the appointed means of gaining all blessings from God. 'All things are possible to him that believeth.'[2] Now, at stated times, when we gather up our thoughts to pray, and draw out our petitions in an orderly and clear manner, the act of faith is likely to be stronger and more earnest; then we realize more perfectly the presence of that God whom we do not see, and Him on whom once all our sins were laid, who bore the weight of our infirmities and sickness once for all, that in all our troubles we might seek Him, and find grace in time of need. Then this world is more out of sight, and we more simply appropriate those blessings, which we have but to claim humbly and they are really ours.

Stated times of prayer, then, are necessary; first, as a means of making the mind sober, and the general temper more religious; secondly, as a means of exercising earnest faith, and thereby of receiving a more certain blessing in answer, than we should otherwise obtain.

Times of Private Prayer   PPS I p. 250–1.   20 December, 1829

1   Matt 6, 6
2   Mark 9, 23

The very object of love is goodness; and all those distinct elements of the moral law, which the typical child, whom I am supposing, more or less consciously loves and approves, – truth, purity, justice, kindness, and the like, – are but shapes and aspects of goodness. And having in his degree a sensibility towards them all, for the sake of them all he is moved to love the Lawgiver, who enjoins them upon him. And, as he can contemplate these qualities and their manifestations under the common name of goodness, he is prepared to think of them as indivisible, correlative, supplementary of each other in one and the same Personality, so that there is no aspect of goodness which God is not; and that the more, because the notion of a perfection embracing all possible excellences, both moral and intellectual, is especially congenial to the mind, and there are in fact intellectual attributes, as well as moral, included in the child's image of God, as above represented.

Apprehension and Assent in Religion. Belief in One God   GA p. 114 (1870)

Eighteenth Sunday of the Year

Eccles. 1, 2. 2, 21–23; Col 3, 1–5. 9–11; Luke 12, 13–21

The Rich Man . . .

. . . 'Hath not God chosen the poor of this world rich in faith, and heirs of that kingdom which He hath promised to them that love Him?'[1] Now, I cite these texts in the way of doctrine, not of precept. Whatever be the line of conduct they prescribe to this or that individual (with which I have nothing to do at present), so far seems clear, that according to the rule of the Gospel, the absence of wealth is, as such, a more blessed and a more Christian state than the possession of it.

The most obvious danger which worldly possessions present to our spiritual welfare is, that they become practically a substitute in our hearts for that One Object to which our supreme devotion is due.

But, in truth, that our Lord meant to speak of riches as being in some sense a calamity to the Christian, is plain, not only from such texts as the foregoing, but from His praises and recommendation on the other hand of poverty. For instance, 'Sell that ye have and give alms; provide yourselves bags which wax not old.' 'If thou wilt be perfect, go sell that thou hast, and give to the poor, and thou shalt have treasure in heaven.' 'Blessed be ye poor: for yours is the kingdom of God.' 'When thou makes a dinner or a supper, call not thy friends, nor thy brethren, neither thy kinsmen, nor thy rich neighbours . . . but . . . call the poor, the maimed, the lame, the blind.'[2] . . .

Money is a sort of creation, and gives the acquirer, even more than the possessor, an imagination of his own power; and tends to make him idolize self. Again, what we have hardly won, we are unwilling to part with; so that a man who has himself made his wealth will commonly be penurious, or at least will not part with it except in exchange for what will reflect credit upon himself, or increase his importance. Even when his conduct is most disinterested and amiable (as in spending for the comfort of those who depend upon him), still this indulgence of self, of pride and worldliness, insinuates itself.

St. Matthew. Danger of Riches   PPS II p. 346–7, 355.   1 February, 1835

1   Jas 2, 5
2   Luke 12, 33; Matt 19, 21

Nineteenth Sunday of the Year

Wisd 18, 6–9; Heb 11, 1–2. 8–19; Luke 12, 32–48

Those whom God finds watching

Now I consider this word *watching*, first used by our Lord, then by the favoured Disciple, then by the two great Apostles, Peter and Paul, is a remarkable word, remarkable because the idea is not so obvious as might appear at first sight, and next because they all inculcate it. We are not simply to believe, but to watch; not simply to love, but to watch; not simply to obey, but to watch; to watch for what? for that great event, Christ's coming. Whether then we consider what is the obvious meaning of the word, or the Object towards which it directs us, we seem to see a special duty enjoined on us, such as does not naturally come into our minds. Most of us have a general idea what is meant by believing, fearing, loving, and obeying; but perhaps we do not contemplate or apprehend what is meant by watching . . .

He watches for Christ who has a sensitive, eager, apprehensive mind; who is awake, alive, quick-sighted, zealous in seeking and honouring Him; who looks out for Him in all that happens, and who would not be surprised, who would not be over-agitated or overwhelmed, if he found that He was coming at once.

And he watches *with* Christ, who, while he looks on to the future, looks back on the past, and does not so contemplate what his Saviour has purchased for him, as to forget what He has suffered for him.

PPS IV p. 321–2, 323.   3 December, 1837

Twentieth Sunday of the Year

Jer 38, 4–6. 8–10; Heb 12, 1–4; Luke 12, 49–53

The Troubles of the Christian

To their surprise, as time goes on, they find that their lot is changed. They find that in one shape or other adversity happens to them. If they refuse to afflict themselves, God afflicts them. One blow falls, they are startled; it passes over, it is well; they expect nothing more. Another comes; they wonder; 'Why is this?' they ask; they think that the first should be their security against the second; they bear it, however; and it passes too. Then a third comes; they almost murmur; they have not yet mastered the great doctrine that endurance is their portion. O simple soul, is it not the law of thy being to endure since thou camest to Christ? Why camest thou but to endure? Why didst thou taste His heavenly feast, but that it might work in thee? Why didst thou kneel beneath His hand, but that He might leave on thee the print of His wounds? Why wonder then that one sorrow does not buy off the next? Does one drop of rain absorb the second? Does the storm cease because it has begun? Understand thy place in God's kingdom, and rejoice, not complain, that in thy day thou hast thy lot with Prophets and Apostles. Envy not the gay and thriving world. Religious persons ask, 'Why are we so marked out for crosses? Others get on in the world; others are prosperous; their schemes turn out well, and their families settle happily; there is no anxiety, no bereavement among them, while the world fights against us.' This is what they sometimes say, though with some exaggeration certainly, for almost all men, sooner or later, have their troubles, and Christians, as well as others, have their continual comforts. But what then, be it ever so true? If so, it is but what was foretold long ago, and even under the Law fulfilled in its degree.

Endurance, The Christian's Portion   PPS V p. 296–7.   3 March, 1839

Twenty-first Sunday of the Year

Isa 66, 18–21; Heb 12, 5–7. 11–13; Luke 13, 22–30

May we be found worthy at the last

Of course we must not press the words of Scripture; we do not know the exact meaning of the word 'chosen;' we do not know what is meant by being saved 'so as by fire';[1] we do not know what is meant by 'few.' But still the few can never mean the many; and to be called without being chosen cannot but be a misery. We know that the man, in the parable, who came to the feast without a wedding garment, was 'cast into outer darkness.' Let us then set at nought the judgment of the many, whether about truth and falsehood, or about ourselves, and let us go by the judgment of that line of Saints, from the Apostles' times downwards, who were ever spoken against in their generation, ever honoured afterwards, – singular in each point of time as it came, but continuous and the same in the line of their history, – ever protesting against the many, ever agreeing with each other. And, in proportion as we attain to their judgment of things, let us pray God to make it live in us; so that at the Last Day, when all veils are removed, we may be found among those who are inwardly what they seem outwardly, – who with Enoch, and Noah, and Abraham, and Moses, and Joshua, and Caleb, and Phineas, and Samuel, and Elijah, and Jeremiah, and Ezekiel, and the Baptist, and St. Paul, have 'borne and had patience, and for His Name-sake laboured and not fainted,'[2] watched in all things, done the work of an Evangelist, fought a good fight, finished their course, kept the faith.

Many Called, Few Chosen   PPS V p. 268–9.   10 September, 1837

---

1   1 Cor 3, 15
2   Rev 2, 3

Twenty-second Sunday of the Year

Sir 3, 17–20. 28–29; Heb 12, 18–19. 22–24; Luke 14, 1. 7–14

The way to mount up is to go down

He says, for instance, to the aspiring, as to His two Apostles, 'Whosoever will be great among you, let him be your minister; and whosoever will be chief among you, let him be your servant; even as the Son of man came not to be ministered unto, but to minister.'[1] Here is our rule. The way to mount up is to go down. Every step we take downward, makes us higher in the kingdom of heaven. Do you desire to be great? make yourselves little. There is a mysterious connexion between real advancement and self-abasement. If you minister to the humble and despised, if you feed the hungry, tend the sick, succour the distressed; if you bear with the froward, submit to insult, endure ingratitude, render good for evil, you are, as by a divine charm, getting power over the world and rising among the creatures. God has established this law. Thus He does His wonderful works. His instruments are poor and despised; the world hardly knows their names, or not at all. They are busied about what the world thinks petty actions, and no one minds them. They are apparently set on no great works; nothing is seen to come of what they do: they seem to fall. Nay, even as regards religious objects which they themselves profess to desire, there is no natural and visible connexion between their doings and sufferings and these desirable ends; but there is an unseen connexion in the kingdom of God. They rise by falling. Plainly so, for no condescension can be so great as that of our Lord *Himself*. Now the more they abase themselves the more *like* they are to Him; and the more like they are to Him, the greater must be their power with Him ...

... instead of loving display, putting ourselves forward, seeking to be noticed, being loud or eager in speech, and bent on having our own way, to be content, nay, to rejoice in being made little of, to perform what to the flesh are servile offices, to think it enough to be barely suffered among men, to be patient under calumny; not to argue, not to judge, not to pronounce censures, unless a plain duty comes in; and all this because our Lord has said that such conduct is the very way to be exalted in His presence.

The Weapons of Saints   PPS VI p. 319–20. 321.   29 October, 1837

1   Matt 20, 26–28

Twenty-third Sunday of the Year

Wisd 9, 13–18; Philem 9–10. 12–17; Luke 14, 25–33

Counting the Cost

He bids you take up your cross; therefore accept the daily opportunities which occur of yielding to others, when you need not yield, and of doing unpleasant services, which you might avoid. He bids those who would be highest, live as the lowest; therefore, turn from ambitious thoughts, and (as far as you religiously may) make resolves against taking on you authority and rule. He bids you sell and give alms; therefore, hate to spend money on yourself. Shut your ears to praise, when it grows loud: set your face like a flint, when the world ridicules, and smile at its threats. Learn to master your heart, when it would burst forth into vehemence, or prolong a barren sorrow, or dissolve into unseasonable tenderness. Curb your tongue, and turn away your eye, lest you fall into temptation. Avoid the dangerous air which relaxes you, and brace yourself upon the heights. Be up at prayer 'a great while before day,'[1] and seek the true, your only bridegroom, 'by night on your bed.'[2] So shall self-denial become natural to you, and a change come over you, gently and imperceptibly; and, like Jacob, you will lie down in the waste, and will soon see Angels, and a way opened for you into heaven.

The Duty of Self-denial PPS VII p. 100–1. 28 March, 1830

---

1 Mark 1, 35
2 S of S 3, 1

Twenty-fourth Sunday of the Year

Exod 32, 7–11. 13–14; 1 Tim 1, 12–17; Luke 15, 1–32

'Rejoice with me . . . '

Would you see how a penitent should come to God? turn to the parable of the Prodigal Son. He, too, had squandered away his birthright, as Esau did. He, too, came for the blessing, like Esau.[1] Yes; but how differently he came! he came with deep confession and self-abasement. He said, 'Father, I have sinned against heaven and before thee, and am no more worthy to be called thy son: make me as one of thy hired servants:' but Esau said, 'Let my father arise, and eat of his son's venison, that thy soul may bless me.' The one came for a son's privileges, the other for a servant's drudgery. The one killed and dressed his venison with his own hand, and enjoyed it not; for the other the fatted calf was prepared, and the ring for his hand, and shoes for his feet, and the best robe, and there was music and dancing.

Life the Season of Repentance   PPS VI p. 21.   15 March, 1840

Cf. 4th Sunday of Lent (C)

---

1   Gen 25. 31. 27, 31

Twenty-fifth Sunday of the Year

Amos 8, 4–7; 1 Tim 2, 1–8; Luke 16, 1–13

The Unjust Steward

And so as regards the Parable of the Steward, on which I am now remarking, fields and market-gardens and woods yield a produce, and are the means of wealth; such as hay, wheat, and other kinds of corn, and various fruits and vegetables in this country; such are olive yards, vineyards, sugar-canes, and other produce of the land abroad. As, then, money creates money, as the land bears bread, wine, and oil, so our souls should yield the due return to God for the many gifts which He has bestowed upon us.

I am speaking of those gifts which belong to our nature, our birth, or our circumstances; gifts of this world. He has given us the means of worshipping Him and doing Him service. He has given us reason, and a certain measure of abilities, more or less. He has given us health, more or less. He has placed us in a certain station of life, high or low. He has given us a certain power of influencing others. He has given us a certain circle of persons, larger or smaller, who depend on us, whom our words and our actions affect for good or for evil, and ought to affect for good. He has given us our share of opportunities of doing good to others. All these are God's gifts to us, and they are given us, not to be wasted, but to be used, to be turned to account. The Steward in the parable wasted them, and was made responsible for his waste. And so in our own case, we may waste them, as most men waste them; nay, worse, we may not only squander them away, we do not know how; but we may actually misapply them, we may use them actually to the injury of Him who has given them to us; but whether we do nothing with them for God, or actually go on to use them to His dishonour and against the interests of truth and religion (and the latter is more likely than the former, for not to do good with them is in fact to do evil), anyhow we shall have one day to answer for our use of them.

Thus the parable before us applies to all of us, as having certain goods committed to us by our Divine Master with a day of reckoning for them in prospect. But this is not all. Charges were brought against the Steward, and his employer called on him to answer them, or rather examined them, and found them well founded. And so it is sometimes with us, that our conscience, which is the voice of God in the soul, upbraids us, brings before us our neglect of duty, the careless, the irreligious, the evil life which we are leading, our disregard of God's commands, glory and worship; and anticipates that judgement which is to come. Now, sometimes this self-accusation leads us to true repentance and change of life – certainly, praise be to God, this is sometimes the case; but more frequently, instead of turning us into the right path, it has the effect of making us go more wrong than we were before.

Stewards and also Sons of God   CS p. 107. 108–9.   8th after Pentecost, 31 July, 1870, The Birmingham Oratory

Twenty-sixth Sunday of the Year

Amos 6, 1. 4–7; 1 Tim 6, 11–16; Luke 16, 19–31

The Rich Man and Lazarus

Look at that poor profligate in the Gospel, look at Dives; do you think he understood that his wealth was to be spent, not on himself, but for the glory of God? – yet for forgetting this, he was lost for ever and ever. I will tell you what he thought, and how he viewed things: – he was a young man, and had succeeded to a good estate, and he determined to enjoy himself. It did not strike him that his wealth had any other use than that of enabling him to take his pleasure. Lazarus lay at his gate; he might have relieved Lazarus; *that* was God's will; but he managed to put conscience aside, and he persuaded himself he should be a fool, if he did not make the most of this world, while he had the means. So he resolved to have his fill of pleasure; and feasting was to his mind a principal part of it. 'He fared sumptuously every day'; 'everything belonging to him was in the best style, as men speak; his house, his furniture, his plate of silver and gold, his attendants, his establishments. Everything was for enjoyment, and for show too; to attract the eyes of the world, and to gain the applause and admiration of his equals, who were the companions of his sins. These companions were doubtless such as became a person of such pretensions; they were fashionable men; a collection of refined, high-bred, haughty men, eating, not gluttonously, but what was rare and costly; delicate, exact, fastidious in their taste, from their very habits of indulgence; not eating for the mere sake of eating, or drinking for the mere sake of drinking, but making a sort of science of their sensuality; sensual, carnal, as flesh and blood can be, with eyes, ears, tongue, steeped in impurity, every thought, look, and sense, witnessing or ministering to the evil one who ruled them; yet, with exquisite correctness of idea and judgment, laying down rules for sinning; – heartless and selfish, high, punctilious, and disdainful in their outward deportment, and shrinking from Lazarus, who lay at the gate, as an eye-sore, who ought for the sake of decency to be put out of the way.

God's Will the End of Life *Mix* p. 113–4 (Discourse 6). 1849

Twenty-seventh Sunday of the Year

Hab 1, 2–3. 2, 2–4; 2 Tim 1, 6–8. 13–14; Luke 17, 5–10

We have done no more than our duty

Let us simply obey God's will, whatever may befall; whether it tend to elate us or to depress us, what is that to us? He can turn all things to our eternal good. He can bless and sanctify even our infirmities. He can lovingly chastise us, if we be puffed up, and He can cheer us when we despond. He can and will exalt us the more we afflict ourselves; and we shall afflict ourselves the more, in true humbleness of mind, the more we really obey Him. Blessed are they who in any matter do His will; and they are thrice blessed who, in what they are doing, are also interesting themselves, as in the case which has been under our consideration, in His special sacramental promises.

Reliance on Religious Observances   PPS IV p. 78.   30 April, 1837

Twenty-eighth Sunday of the Year

2 Kgs 5, 14–17; 2 Tim 2, 8–13; Luke 17, 11–19

Giving thanks to God

We are not our own, any more than what we possess is our own. We did not make ourselves; we cannot be supreme over ourselves. We cannot be our own masters. We are God's property by creation, by redemption, by regeneration. He has a triple claim upon us. Is it not our happiness thus to view the matter? Is it any happiness, or any comfort, to consider that we are our own? It may be thought so by the young and prosperous. These may think it a great thing to have everything, as they suppose, their own way, – to depend on no one, – to have to think of nothing out of sight, – to be without the irksomeness of continual acknowledgement, continual prayer, continual reference of what they do to the will of another. But as time goes on, they, as all men, will find that independence was not made for man – that it is an unnatural state – may do for a while, but will not carry us on safely to the end. No, we are creatures; and, as being such, we have two duties, to be resigned and to be thankful.

Remembrance of past Mercies   PPS V p. 83–4.   22 September, 1838

Twenty-ninth Sunday of the Year

Exod 17, 8–13; 2 Tim 3, 14–4, 2; Luke 18, 1–8

The Power of Prayer

A man cannot really be religious one hour, and not religious the next. We might as well say he could be in a state of good health one hour, and in bad health the next. A man who is religious, is religious morning, noon, and night; his religion is a certain character, a mould in which his thoughts, words, and actions are cast, all forming parts of one and the same whole. He sees God in all things; every course of action he directs towards those spiritual objects which God has revealed to him; every occurrence of the day, every event, every person met with, all news which he hears, he measures by the standard of God's will. And a person who does this may be said almost literally to pray without ceasing; for, knowing himself to be in God's presence, he is continually led to address Him reverently, whom he sets always before him, in the inward language of prayer and praise, of humble confession and joyful trust.

All this, I say, any thoughtful man acknowledges from mere natural reason. To be religious is, in other words, to have the habit of prayer, or to pray always. This is what Scripture means by doing all things to God's glory; that is, so placing God's presence and will before us, and so consistently acting with a reference to Him, that all we do becomes one body and course of obedience, witnessing without ceasing to Him who made us, and whose servants we are; and in its separate parts promoting more or less directly His glory, according as each particular thing we happen to be doing admits more or less of a religious character.

Mental Prayer   PPS VII p. 205–6.   13 December, 1829

Thirtieth Sunday of the Year

Sir 35, 12–14. 16–19; 2 Tim 4, 6–8. 16–18; Luke 18, 9–14

The Pharisee and the Tax Collector

Samuel was a little child who had never fallen away from God, but by His grace had ever served Him. Let us take a very different instance, the instance of a penitent sinner as set before us in the parable of the Publican and Pharisee. I need hardly say which of the two was the most pleasing to God – the Publican; whereas the Pharisee was not accepted by Him. Now what did the Pharisee do? He did not even go so far as to behave in an unseemly, extravagant way: he was grave and solemn, and yet what he did was enough to displease God, because he took too much upon himself, and made too much of himself. Though grave and solemn, he was not reverent; he spoke in a haughty, proud way, and made a long sentence, thanking God that he was not as other men are, and despising the Publican. Such was the behaviour of the Pharisee; but the Publican behaved very differently. Observe how he came to worship God; 'he stood afar off; he lift not up so much as his eyes unto heaven, but smote upon his breast, saying, God be merciful to me a sinner.' You see his words were few, and almost broken, and his whole conduct humble and reverent; he felt that God was in heaven, he upon earth, God All-holy and Almighty, and he a poor sinner.

Now all of us are sinners, all of us have need to come to God as the Publican did; every one, if he does but search his heart, and watch his conduct, and try to do his duty, will find himself to be full of sins which provoke God's wrath. I do not mean to say that all men are equally sinners; some are wilful sinners, and of them there is no hope, till they repent; others sin, but they try to avoid sinning, pray to God to make them better, and come to Church to be made better; but all men are quite sinners enough to make it their duty to behave as the Publican. Every one ought to come into Church as the Publican did, to say in his heart, 'Lord, I am not worthy to enter this sacred place; my only plea for coming is the merits of Jesus Christ my Saviour.'

Reverence in Worship   PPS VIII p. 6–7.   30 October, 1836

Thirty-first Sunday of the Year

Wisd 11, 22–12, 2; 2 Thess 1, 11–2, 2; Luke 19, 1–10

Christ at the House of Zacchaeus

And, first, let it be observed, from the beginning, the greatest rite of religion has been a feast;[1] the partaking of God's bounties, in the way of nature, has been consecrated to a more immediate communion with God Himself. For instance, when Isaac was weaned, Abraham 'made a great feast,' and then it was that Sarah prophesied; 'Cast out this bondwoman and her son,' she said, prophesying the introduction of the spirit, grace, and truth, which the Gospel contains, instead of the bondage of the outward forms of the Law. Again, it was at a feast of savoury meat that the spirit of prophecy came upon Isaac, and he blessed Jacob. In like manner the first beginning of our Lord's miracles was at a marriage feast, when He changed water into wine; and when St. Matthew was converted he entertained our Lord at a feast. At a feast, too, our Lord allowed the penitent woman to wash with tears and anoint His feet, and pronounced her forgiveness; and at a feast, before His passion, He allowed Mary to anoint them with costly ointment, and to wipe them with her hair. Thus with our Lord, and with the Patriarchs, a feast was a time of grace; so much so, that He was said by the Pharisees to come eating and drinking, to be 'a winebibber and gluttonous, a friend of publicans and sinners.'[2]

The Gospel Feast   PPS VII p. 168–9.   20/27 May, 1838

---

1   Gen. 21, 10
2   Matt.11,19; Luke 7, 34

Thirty-second Sunday of the Year

2 Macc 7, 1–2. 9–14; 2 Thess 2, 16–3, 5; Luke 20, 27–38

The God of Abraham, Isaac and Jacob

When God called Himself the God of Abraham, Isaac, and Jacob, He implied that those holy patriarchs were still alive, though they were no more seen on earth. This may seem evident at first sight; but it may be asked, how the text proves that their *bodies* would live; for, if their *souls* were still living, that would be enough to account for their being still called in the Book of Exodus servants of God . . .

. . . Our Blessed Lord seems to tell us, that in some sense or other Abraham's *body* might be considered still alive as a pledge of his resurrection, though it was dead in the common sense in which we apply the word. His announcement is, Abraham *shall* rise from the dead, because in truth, he *is* still alive. He cannot in the end be held under the power of the grave, more than a sleeping man can be kept from waking. Abraham is still alive in the dust, though not risen thence. He is alive because all God's saints live to Him, though they seem to perish . . .

God graciously called Himself *the God of Abraham*. He did not say the God of Abraham's soul, but simply of *Abraham*. He blest Abraham, and He gave him eternal life; not to his soul only without his body, but to Abraham as one man. And so He is *our* God, and it is not given us to distinguish between what He does for our different natures, spiritual and material. These are mere words; each of us may feel himself to be one, and that one being, in all its substantial parts, and attributes, will never die.

The Resurrection of the Body   PPS I p. 272. 273–4.   22 April, 1832

Thirty-third Sunday of the Year

Mal 3, 19–20; 2 Thess 3, 7–12; Luke 21, 5–19

In Persecution the Church begins and in Persecution she ends

We have been so accustomed to hear of the persecutions of the
Church, both from the New Testament and from the history of
Christianity, that it is much if we have not at length come to regard
the account of them as words of course, to speak of them without
understanding what we say, and to receive nò practical benefit from
having been told of them; much less are we likely to take them for
what they really are, a characteristic mark of Christ's Church. They
are not indeed the necessary lot of the Church, but at least one of her
appropriate badges; so that, on the whole, looking at the course of
history, you might set down persecution as one of the peculiarities by
which you recognize her. And our Lord seems to intimate how
becoming, how natural persecution is to the Church, by placing it
among His Beatitudes. 'Blessed are they who are persecuted for
righteousness sake, for theirs is the kingdom of heaven'; giving it the
same high and honourable rank in the assemblage of evangelical
graces, which the Sabbath holds among the Ten Commandments, –
I mean, as a sort of sign and token of His followers, and, as such,
placed in the moral code, though in itself external to it.

He seems to show us this in another way, viz., by intimating to us
the fact, that in persecution the Church begins and in persecution she
ends. He left her in persecution, and He will find her in persecution.
He recognizes her as His own, – He framed, and He will claim her,
– as a persecuted Church, bearing His Cross. And that awful relic of
Him which He gave her, and which she is found possessed of at the
end, she cannot have lost by the way . . .

This alone I will say, in conclusion, as I have already said several
times, that such meditations as these may be turned to good account.
It will act as a curb upon our self-willed, selfish hearts, to believe that
a persecution is in store for the Church, whether or not it comes in our
days. Surely, with this prospect before us, we cannot bear to give
ourselves up to thoughts of ease and comfort, of making money,
settling well, or rising in the world. Surely, with this prospect before
us, we cannot but feel that we are, what all Christians really are in the
best estate (nay, rather would wish to be, had they their will, if they
be Christians in heart), pilgrims, watchers waiting for the morning,

waiting for the light, eagerly straining our eyes for the first dawn of day — looking out for our Lord's coming, His glorious advent, when He will end the reign of sin and wickedness, accomplish the number of His elect, and perfect those who at present struggle with infirmity, yet in their hearts love and obey Him.

The Patristical Idea of Antichrist   DA p. 93–4. 106 (Tract 85) 21 September, 1838

Our Lord Jesus Christ, Universal King (34th Sunday)

2 Sam 5, 1–3; Col 1, 12–20; Luke 23, 35–43

The Royal Pardon from the Throne of the Cross

Consider the deep and serene compassion which led Him to pray for those who crucified Him; His solicitous care of His Mother; and His pardoning words addressed to the robber who suffered with Him. And so, when He said, 'It is finished,' He showed that He was still contemplating, with a clear intellect, 'the travail of His soul, and was satisfied'; and in the solemn surrender of Himself into His Father's hand, He showed where His mind rested in the midst of its darkness. Even when He seemed to be thinking of Himself, and said, 'I thirst,' He really was regarding the world of Prophecy, and was bent on vindicating, to the very letter, the divine announcements concerning Him. Thus, upon the Cross itself, we discern in Him the mercy of a Messenger from heaven, the love and grace of a Saviour, the dutifulness of a Son, the faith of a created nature, and the zeal of a servant of God . . .

. . . Who, on the other hand, does not at least perceive that all the glare and gaudiness of this world, its excitements, its keenly-pursued goods, its successes and its transports, its pomps and its luxuries, are not in character with that pale and solemn scene which faith must ever have in its eye? What Christian will not own that to 'reign as kings,' and to be 'full,' is not his calling; so as to derive comfort in the hour of sickness, or bereavement, or other affliction, from the thought that he is now in his own place, if he be Christ's, in his true home, the sepulchre in which his Lord was laid? So deeply have His Saints felt this, that when times were peaceful, and the Church was in safety, they could not rest in the lap of ease, and have secured to themselves hardnesses, lest the world should corrupt them.

Bodily Suffering   PPS III p. 149, 151.   3 May, 1835

Part II:
Solemnities & Holydays of Obligation

Solemnities & Holydays of Obligation

February 2	The Presentation of the Lord
March 17	St. Patrick
March 19	St. Joseph
March 25	The Annunciation of the Lord
June 24	The Birth of John the Baptist
June 29	St. Peter and St. Paul, Apostles
August 6	The Transfiguration of the Lord (readings for years A, B and C)
August 15	The Assumption of the Blessed Virgin Mary
September 14	The Triumph of the Cross
November 1	All Saints
November 9	The Dedication of the Lateran Basilica
December 8	The Immaculate Conception of the Blessed Virgin Mary

* The Feasts of The Body and Blood of Christ and the Sacred Heart have different Scripture texts for each year and can be found after the readings for Trinity Sunday.

2 February, The Presentation of the Lord

Mal 3, 1–4; Heb 2, 14–18; Luke 2, 22–40

He came to his own Temple

The infant in arms was the Saviour of the world, the rightful heir, come in disguise of a stranger to visit His own house. The Scripture has said, 'The Lord whom ye seek shall suddenly come to His Temple: but who may abide the day of His coming, and who may stand when He appeareth?' He had now taken possession. And further, the old man who took the child in his arms, had upon him the gifts of the Holy Ghost, had been promised the blessed sight of his Lord before his death, came into the Temple by heavenly guidance, and now had within him thoughts unutterable, of joy, thankfulness, and hope, strangely mixed with awe, fear, painful wonder, and 'bitterness of spirit' Anna too, the woman of fourscore and four years, was a prophetess; and the bystanders, to whom she spoke, were the true Israel, who were looking out in faith for the predicted redemption of mankind, those who (in the words of the prophecy) 'sought' and in prospect 'delighted' in the 'Messenger' of God's covenant of mercy. 'The glory of this latter House shall be greater than of the former,'[1] was the announcement made in another prophecy. Behold the glory; a little child and his parents, two aged persons, and a congregation without name or memorial. 'The kingdom of God cometh not with observation.'

Purification of the Blessed Virgin. Secrecy of Divine Visitations   PPS II p. 110
2 February, 1831.

---

1   Hag. 2, 9

In Scripture we read not of all the good men who ever were, only of a few, viz. those in whom God's name was especially honoured. Doubtless there have been many widows in Israel, serving God in fastings and prayers, like Anna; but she only is mentioned in Scripture, as being in a situation to glorify the Lord Jesus. She spoke of the Infant Saviour 'to all them that looked for redemption in Jerusalem.'

Annunciation of the Blessed Virgin. The Reverence due to Her.
PPS II p. 133.   25 March, 1832

17 March, St. Patrick

Jer 1, 4–9; Acts 13, 46–49; Luke 10, 1–12. 17–20

St Patrick and the Irish

Well might so great a Saint say, at the end of his days 'Come, Lord Jesus!' as those who are weary of the night, and wait for the morning. All his thoughts, all his contemplations, desires, and hopes, were stored in the invisible world; and death, when it came, brought back to him the sight of what he had worshipped, what he had loved, what he had held intercourse with, in years long past away. Then, when again brought into the presence of what he had lost, how would remembrance revive, and familiar thoughts long buried come to life! Who shall dare to describe the blessedness of those who find all their pledges safe returned to them, all their ventures abundantly and beyond measure satisfied?

Alas! that we, my brethren, have not more of this high and unearthly spirit! How is it that we are so contented with things as they are, – that we are so willing to be let alone, and to enjoy this life, – that we make such excuses, if any one presses on us the necessity of something higher, the duty of bearing the Cross, if we would earn the Crown, of the Lord Jesus Christ?

I repeat it; what are our ventures and risks upon the truth of His word? for He says expressly, 'Every one that hath forsaken houses, or brethren, or sisters, or father, or mother, or wife, or children, or lands, for My Name's sake, shall receive an hundred-fold, and shall inherit everlasting life. But many that are first shall be last; and the last shall be first.'[1]

The Ventures of Faith   PPS IV p. 306.   21 February, 1836

---

1   Matt 19, 29. 30

I go further still. If I do homage to the many virtues and gifts of the Irish people, and am zealous for their full development, it is not simply for the sake of themselves, but because the name of Ireland ever has been, and, I believe, ever will be, associated with the Catholic Faith, and because, in doing any service, however poor it may be, to Ireland, a man is ministering, in his own place and measure, to the cause of the Holy Roman Apostolic Church.

Discipline of Mind.   Idea p. 482.   November 1858

Rome was the missionary centre, from which each of them in turn received the revealed doctrine; from Rome Patrick first, and then Augustine, received both their mission and their tradition; and the grace and merits of those two apostles so wrought in the countries which they respectively converted, that those countries became rivals of each other in sanctity, learning and zealous works. The Irish saints are said to be more than can be counted; the English are remarkable for being clustered into families, and those of royal lineage.

Northmen and Normans in England and Ireland   HS III p. 265.   May 1859

19 March, St. Joseph, Husband of the Blessed Virgin Mary

2 Sam 7, 4−5. 12−14. 16; Rom 4, 13, 16−18. 22; Matt 1, 16. 18−21. 24

'And Jacob was the Father of Joseph, the Husband of Mary'

St. Joseph furnishes the most striking instance of this remark; here is the clearest of instances of the distinction between doctrine and devotion. Who, from his prerogatives and the testimony on which they come to us, had a greater claim to receive an early recognition, among the faithful than he? A Saint of Scripture, the foster-father of our Lord, he was an object of the universal and absolute faith of the Christian world from the first, yet the devotion to him is comparatively of late date. When once it began, men seemed surprised that it had not been thought of before; and now, they hold him next to the Blessed Virgin in their religious affection and veneration.

Belief of Catholics that she is the Second Eve   *Diff* II p. 30−1 (Letter to Pusey) 1864

And when He had reached twelve years old, at the age when the young may expect to be separated from their parents, He had only become more intimately one with them, for we are told that 'He went down with them, and came to Nazareth, and was subject upto them.' Eighteen years had passed away since this occurred. St. Joseph (as it seems) had been taken to his rest. Mary remained; but from Mary, His Mother, He must now part, for the three years of His ministry. He had gently intimated this to her at the very time of His becoming subject to her, intimated that His heavenly Father's work was a higher call than any earthly duty. 'Wist ye not,' He said, when found in the Temple, 'that I must be about My Father's business?' The time was now come when this was to be fulfilled ...

Our Lord's Last Supper and His First   SD p. 32.   26 February, 1843

25 March, The Annunciation of the Lord

Isa 7, 10–14. 8, 10; Heb 10, 4–10; Luke 1, 26–38

'. . . So the Child will be Holy and will be called Son of God'

This is the great Mystery which we are now celebrating, of which mercy is the beginning, and sanctity the end: according to the Psalm, 'Righteousness and peace have kissed each other.'[1] He who is all purity came to an impure race to raise them to His purity. He, the brightness of God's glory, came in a body of flesh, which was pure and holy as Himself, 'without spot, or wrinkle, or any such thing, but holy and without blemish';[2] and this He did for our sake, 'that we might be partakers of His holiness.' He needed not a human nature for Himself, – He was all-perfect in His original Divine nature; but He took upon Himself what was ours for the sake of us. He who 'hath made of one blood all nations of men,' so that in the sin of one all sinned, and in the death of one all died, He came in that very nature of Adam, in order to communicate to us that nature as it is in His Person, that 'our sinful bodies might be made clean by His Body, and our souls washed though His most precious Blood'; to make us partakers of the Divine nature; to sow the seed of eternal life in our hearts; and to raise us from 'the corruption that is in the world through lust,' to that immaculate purity and that fulness of grace which is in Him. He who is the first principle and pattern of all things, came to be the beginning and pattern of human kind, the first-born of the whole creation. He, who is the everlasting Light, became the Light of men; He, who is the Life from eternity, became the Life of a race dead in sin; He, who is the word of God, came to be a spiritual Word, 'dwelling richly in our hearts,' an 'engrafted Word, which is able to save our souls';[3] He, who is the co-equal Son of the Father, came to be the Son of God in our flesh, that He might raise us also to the adoption of sons, and might be first among many brethren. And this is the reason why the Collect for the season, after speaking of our Lord as the Only-begotten Son, and born in our nature of a pure Virgin, proceeds to speak of our new birth and adopted sonship, and renewal by the grace of the Holy Ghost.

The Mystery of Godliness   PPS V p. 92–3.   26 March, 1837

24 June, The Birth of St John the Baptist   Vigil Mass

Jer 1, 4–10; 1 Pet 1, 8–12; Luke 1, 5–17

'John came to you, a Pattern of True Righteousness'

When then it is said, as it so often is said in Scripture, that the righteous are righteous 'before God,' this means that their righteousness is not merely the name or semblance of righteousness, nor righteousness up to an earthly standard, but a real and true righteousness which approves itself to God. They are able to stand before God and yet not be condemned. They are not sinners before God, but they are righteous before God, and bear His scrutiny. By nature no one can stand in His presence. 'All the world becomes guilty *before God.*' 'By the deeds of the Law no flesh shall be justified in *His sight.' How* then are we able to *come before Him?* How shall we stand in His sight? The answer is given us in the Old Testament, in the words of Balaam to Balak. Balak asked, 'Wherewith shall I come before the Lord, and bow myself before the High God?' and the answer was, 'He hath showed thee, O man, what is good; and what doth the Lord require of thee, but to do justly, and to love mercy, and to walk humbly with thy God?' Or again, the answer may be given in the words of Zacharias, who blesses the Lord God of Israel for fulfilling His promise, and enabling us to come into His presence to 'serve Him, *without fear,* in holiness and righteousness *before Him.*' And accordingly, to come to the case of individuals, Noah, even before the Gospel times, is said to have 'found grace in the eyes of the Lord.' Why? Because, in the words of Almighty God to him, *'Thee* have I seen righteous *before Me.*'!

The Law of the Spirit PPS V p. 153. 12 January, 1840

29 June,

Acts 12, 1 – 11; 2 Tim 4, 6 – 8. 17 – 18; Matt 16, 13 – 19

'You are Peter and on this Rock I will build my Church'

When in St. Matthew He spoke of St. Peter as the rock, He did not speak – it was not His will then to speak – of St. Peter as the shepherd, but he thought it very remarkable, and a point demanding very great consideration, that there was one passage they knew, in which Our Lord committed His sheep to one of His Apostles. He says, 'Feed My sheep.' He said it to St. Peter. He (His Eminence) did not on consideration find anything parallel to that in the case of the other Apostles. There was that great characteristic title of Almighty God, that office which He exercised towards His elected people, towards those whom He described as His sheep. That title, that office, He delegated on His going away to one of His Apostles, and he was St. Peter. He saw nothing like such a delegation of so especial and so peculiar an office to any other Apostle. The Church acknowledged St. Peter as the Pastor, and according to the law of the Church, the rule of the Church, the Shepherd; and when they came to look back upon the passage in which He thus delegated His office, which made St. Peter what he might call a Vicegerent or Vicar, there seemed to be occasion for it, for He was going away; therefore, He did it. When He was going away they knew that He said, 'All power is given to Me in Heaven and earth.' He would be with His Apostles till the end of time – always. It did not seem to accord. St. Peter had not neglected his sheep, for the sheep had not yet been given. It was sometimes said it was the restoration of St. Peter after his fall; his fall was the denial of his Lord, and had no connexion with the bringing of others into the Church, which Our Lord emphasised three times in those words in which He gave him the charge, and which had some correspondence to St. Peter's three denials; but still there was involved, notwithstanding the circumstances of his denial, the charge to St. Peter, and not to the Apostles generally. Then it seemed remarkable that that high gift should have been given in the Old Testament. They knew that it was given by God to David, who became the Vicegerent of Almighty God. It seemed to him that that passage was parallel to that which regarded St. Peter. They knew that Our Lord had a treble office: He was the king, the prophet, and the priest, and the word shepherd combined all these things, and was explained in the Psalm that he had read to them. He had the office of ruling, He had the office of feeding, because they knew that a shepherd fed his sheep; and thirdly, in those countries they knew that the shepherd's office was one full of great danger. He had to defend his sheep from the wild beasts. As in the case of David, he had to take care of his pastorate, and to defend his sheep from the inclement weather. In the case of Jacob, there was a great deal of danger in the office of shepherd. It was an office which would really be given to the representative of Our Lord. It was something that seemed to him different from any other office which was given to anyone else under the new covenant. They were all there Catholics, and they all believed it, and there was no need to say this in order to strengthen their faith; but it was pleasant and a cause of thanksgiving that they could contemplate and consider this, which was a matter of faith. The Apostles died off; and, therefore, there must in the nature of things be a succession, and then he wanted to know, if Bishops were to succeed, why was not the head of the Apostles to have a succession? Somewhere they must look for that succession; that seemed plain. When they had reason to believe a thing it was a great confirmation to find from the nature of the case that it must be according to their apprehension. It must be considered that no large body could exist without a head.

Sayings p. 60–61. 23 May, 1880 – in S. Aloysius, Oxford.

The voice of Peter is now, as it ever has been, a real authority, infallible when it teaches, prosperous when it commands, ever taking the lead wisely and distinctly in its own province, adding certainty to what is probable, and persuasion to what is certain. Before it speaks, the most saintly may mistake; and after it has spoken, the most gifted must obey.

Peter is no recluse, no abstracted student, no dreamer about the past, no doter upon the dead and gone, no projector of the visionary. Peter for eighteen hundred years has lived in the world; he has seen all fortunes, he has encountered all adversaries, he has shaped himself for all emergencies. If there ever was a power on earth who had an eye for the times, who has confirmed himself to the practicable, and has been happy in his anticipations, whose words have been deeds, and whose commands prophecies, such is he in the history of ages, who sits from generation to generation in the Chair of the Apostles, as the Vicar of Christ and Doctor of His Church.

Cathedra sempiterna. *Campaign* p. 211–212

6 August, The Transfiguration of the Lord

Dan 7, 9-10. 13-14; 2 Pet 1, 16-19; Matt, 17, 1-9

'His Face shone like the Sun ... '

Such was the surprise, such the transport, which came upon the favoured disciples, whom on one occasion our Lord took up with Him to the mountain's top. He left the sick world, the tormented, restless multitude, at its foot, and He took them up, and was transfigured before them. 'His face did shine as the sun, and His raiment was white as the light'; and they lifted their eyes, and saw on either side of Him a bright form; − these were two Saints of the elder covenant, Moses and Elias, who were conversing with Him. How truly was this a glimpse of Heaven! the holy Apostles were introduced into a new range of ideas, into a new sphere of contemplation, till St. Peter, overcome by the vision, cried out, 'Lord, it is good to be here; and let us make three tabernacles'. He would fain have kept those heavenly glories always with him; everything on earth, the brightest, the fairest, the noblest, paled and dwindled away, and turned to corruption before them; its most substantial good was vanity, its richest gain was dross, its keenest joy a weariness, and its sin a loathsomeness and abomination. And such as this in its measure is the contrast, to which the awakened soul is witness, between the objects of its admiration and pursuit in its natural state, and those which burst upon it when it has entered into communion with the Church Invisible, when it has come 'to Mount Sion, and to the city of the Living God, the heavenly Jerusalem, and to a company of many thousand Angels, and to the Church of the first-born, who are enrolled in heaven, and to God the Judge of all, and to the spirits of the just now perfected, and to Jesus the Mediator of the New Testatment'.[1]

Saintliness the Standard of Christian Principle   *Mix* p. 92−3 (Discourse 5) 1849

Cf. also 2nd Sunday of Lent A, B, C.

1   Heb 12, 24

6 August, The Transfiguration of the Lord

Dan 7, 9 – 10. 13 – 14; 2 Pet 1, 16 – 19; Mark 9, 2 – 10

'They saw his Glory'

But He was pleased to reveal this high truth more explicitly on a subsequent occasion; I mean in His Transfiguration. To many persons this portion of the Sacred History may have appeared without object or meaning. It was, in one sense, a miracle; yet it had no beneficent purpose or lasting consequence, as is usual with our Lord's miracles, and it took place in private. But, surely, it is of a doctrinal nature, being nothing less than a figurative exhibition of the blessed truth contained in the texts under review, a vision of the glorious Kingdom which He set up on the earth on His coming. He said to His apostles, 'I tell you of a truth, there be some standing here which shall not taste of death till they *see the Kingdom of God*.' Then, 'after six days Jesus taketh Peter, James, and John his brother, and bringeth them up into a high mountain apart, and was transfigured before them. And as He prayed the fashion of His countenance was altered, and His raiment was white and glistening. And His face did shine as the sun, and His raiment was white as the light … And behold there talked with Him two men, which were Moses and Elias, who appeared in glory … But Peter and they that were with him were heavy with sleep; and when they were awake, *they saw His glory*.' Such is the Kingdom of God; Christ the centre of it, His glory the light of it, the Just made perfect His companions, and the Apostles His witnesses to their brethren. It realizes what the ancient Saints saw by glimpses – Jacob at Bethel, Moses on Sinai.

The Gift of the Spirit   PPS III p. 265 – 6.   8 November, 1835

Cf. also 2nd Sunday of Lent A, B, C.

6 August, The Transfiguration of the Lord

Dan 7, 9–10. 13–14; 2 Pet 1, 16–19; Luke 9, 28–36

'. . . Speaking of his Passing which he was to accomplish in Jerusalem'

We see the same law, as it may be called, of Divine Providence in other cases also. Consider, for instance, how the prospect of our Lord's passion opens upon the apostles in the sacred history. Where did they hear of it? 'Moses and Elias on the mountain appeared with Him in glory, and spake of His decease, which He should accomplish at Jerusalem.'[1] That is, the season of His bitter trial was preceded by a short gleam of the glory which was to be, when He was suddenly transfigured, 'and the fashion of His countenance was altered, and His raiment was white and glistering.'[2] And with this glory in prospect, our Lord abhorred not to die: as it is written, 'Who for the joy that was set before Him, endured the Cross, despising the shame.'
    Again, He forewarned His Apostles that they in like manner should be persecuted for righteousness' sake, and be afflicted and delivered up, and hated and killed. Such was to be their life in this world, 'that if in this world only they had had hope in Christ, they had been of all men most miserable.'[3] Well then, observe, their trial too was preceded by a season of peace and pleasantness, in anticipation of their future reward; for before the day of Pentecost, for forty days Christ was with them, soothing, comforting, confirming them, 'and speaking of the things pertaining unto the kingdom of God.'[4] As Moses stood on the Mount and saw the promised land and all its riches, and yet Joshua had to fight many battles before he got possession, so did the Apostles, before descending into the valley of the shadow of death, whence nought of heaven was to be seen, stand upon the heights, and look over that valley, which they had to cross, to the city of the living God beyond it.

The Season of Epiphany   PPS VII p. 81–2.   17 January, 1841

1   Luke 9, 30. 31
2   Luke 9, 29
3   1Cor 15, 19
4   Acts 1, 3

Cf. also 2nd Sunday of Lent A, B, C.

15 August, The Assumption of the Blessed Virgin Mary

Rev 11, 19–12, 1–6. 10; 1 Cor 15, 20–26; Luke 1, 39–56

'All Generations will call me Blessed'

She died, but her death was a mere fact, not an effect; and, when it was over, it ceased to be. She died that she might live, she died as a matter of form or (as I may call it) an observance, in order to fulfil, what is called, the debt of nature, – not primarily for herself or because of sin, but to submit herself to her condition, to glorify God, to do what her Son did; not however as her Son and Saviour, with any suffering for any special end; not with a martyr's death, for her martyrdom had been in living; not as an atonement, for man could not make it, and One had made it, and made it for all ...

The Glories of Mary   Mix p. 372–3 (Discourse 18) 1849

He condescended 'not to abhor the Virgin's womb'?[1] Is it surprising then that on the one hand she should be immaculate in her Conception? or on the other that she should be honoured with an Assumption, and exalted as a queen with a crown of twelve stars, with the rulers of day and night to do her service? Men sometimes wonder that we call her Mother of life, of mercy, of salvation; what are all these titles compared to that one name, Mother of God?

Belief of Catholics that she is Theotokos   Diff II p. 63 (Letter to Pusey) 1864

1   Te Deum laudamus

By her Assumption is meant that not only her soul, but her body also, was taken up to heaven upon her death, so that there was no long period of her sleeping in the grave, as is the case with others, even great Saints, who wait for the last day for the resurrection of their bodies.

One reason for believing in our Lady's Assumption is that her Divine Son loved her too much to let her body remain in the grave. A second reason − that now before us − is this, that she was not only dear to our Lord as a mother is dear to a son, but also that she was so transcendently holy, so full, so overflowing with grace. Adam and Eve were created upright and sinless, and had a large measure of God's grace bestowed upon them; and, in consequence, their bodies would never have crumbled into dust, had they not sinned; upon which it was said to them. 'Dust thou art, and unto dust thou shalt return.'

MD p. 93

14 September, The Triumph of the Cross

Num 21, 4–9; Phil 2, 6–11; John 3, 13–17

Lifted up on the Cross

Let us look upon Him who was lifted up that He might draw us to Him; and, by being drawn one and all to Him, let us be drawn to each other, so that we may understand and feel that He has redeemed us one and all, and that, unless we love one another, we cannot really have love to Him who laid down His life for us.

The Incarnate Son, a Sufferer and Sacrifice   PPS VI p. 70.   1 April, 1836

Again: look at misery, look at poverty and destitution, look at oppression and captivity; go where food is scanty, and lodging unhealthy. Consider pain and suffering, diseases long or violent, all that is frightful and revolting. Would you know how to rate all these? gaze upon the Cross.

Thus in the Cross, and Him who hung upon it, all things meet; all things subserve it, all things need it. It is their centre and their interpretation. For He was lifted up upon it, that He might draw all men and all things unto Him.

But it will be said, that the view which the Cross of Christ imparts to us of human life and of the world, is not that which we should take, if left to ourselves; that it is not an obvious view; that if we look at things on their surface, they are far more bright and sunny than they appear when viewed in the light which this season casts upon them. The world seems made for the enjoyment of just such a being as man, and man is put into it. He has the *capacity* of enjoyment, and the world supplies the *means*. How natural this, what a simple as well as pleasant philosophy, yet how different from that of the Cross!

The Cross of Christ the Measure of the World   PPS VI p. 86.   9 April, 1841

1 November, All Saints

Rev 7, 2–4. 9–14; 1 John 3, 1–3; Matt 5, 1–12

The Cloud of Witnesses

So many were the wonderful works which our Saviour did on earth, that not even the world itself could have contained the books recording them. Nor have His marvels been less since He ascended on high; – those works of higher grace and more abiding fruit, wrought in the souls of men, from the first hour till now, – the captives of His power, the ransomed heirs of His kingdom, whom He has called by His Spirit working in due season, and led on from strength to strength till they appear before His face in Zion. Surely not even the world itself could contain the records of His love, the history of those many Saints, that 'cloud of Witnesses,'[1] whom we to-day celebrate, His purchased possession in every age! We crowd these all up into one day; we mingle together in the brief remembrance of an hour all the choicest deeds, the holiest lives, the noblest labours, the most precious sufferings, which the sun ever saw. Even the least of those Saints were the contemplation of many days, – even the names of them, if read in our Service, would outrun many settings and risings of the light, – even one passage in the life of one of them were more than sufficient for a long discourse. 'Who can count the dust of Jacob, and the number of the fourth part of Israel?'[2] Martyrs and Confessors, Rulers and Doctors of the Church, devoted Ministers and Religious brethren, kings of the earth and all people, princes and judges of the earth, young men and maidens, old men and children, the first fruits of all ranks, ages, and callings, gathered each in his own time into the paradise of God.

All Saints   PPS II p. 393–4.   30 November, 1831

---

1   Heb 12, 1
2   Num 23, 10

9 November, The Dedication of the Lateran Basilica

Ezek 47, 1–2. 8–9. 12; 1 Cor 3, 9–11. 16–17; John 2, 13–22

'He was speaking of the Sanctuary which was his Body . . .'

And so again the Jewish Temple was in one sense inhabited by the presence of God, which came down upon it at Solomon's Prayer. This was a type of our Lord's manhood dwelt in by the Word of God as a Temple; still, with this essential difference, that the Jewish Temple was perishable, and again the Divine Presence might recede from it. There was no real unity between the one and the other; they were separable. But Christ says to the Jews of His own body, 'Destroy this Temple and I will raise it in three days'; implying in these words such a unity between the Godhead and the manhood, that there could be no real separation, no dissolution. Even when His body was dead, the Divine Nature was one with it; in like manner it was one with His soul in paradise. Soul and body were really one with the Eternal Word, – not one in name only, – one never to be divided. Therefore Scripture says that He rose again 'according to the Spirit of holiness'; and 'that it was not possible that He should be holden of death.'[1]

Christmas Day. The Incarnation   PPS II p. 34.   25 December, 1834

---

1   Rom 1, 4; Acts 2, 24

8 December, The Immaculate Conception of the Blessed Virgin Mary

Gen 3, 9–15. 20; Eph 1, 3–6. 11–12; Luke 1, 26–38

'Behold the Handmaid of the Lord'

It is then an integral portion of the Faith fixed by Ecumenical Council, a portion of it which you hold as well as I, that the Blessed Virgin is Theotokos, Deipara, or Mother of God;[1] and this word, when thus used, carries with it no admixture of rhetoric, no taint of extravagant affection, – it has nothing else but a well-weighed, grave, dogmatic sense, which corresponds and is adequate to its sound. It intends to express that God is her Son, as truly as any one of us is the son of his own mother. If this be so, what can be said of any creature whatever, which may not be said of her? what can be said too much, so that it does not compromise the attributes of the Creator? He indeed might have created a being more perfect, more admirable, than she is; He might have endued that being, so created, with a richer grant of grace, of power, of blessedness: but in one respect she surpasses all even possible creations, viz., that she is Mother of her Creator. It is this awful title, which both illustrates and connects together the two prerogatives of Mary, on which I have been lately enlarging, her sanctity and her greatness. It is the issue of her sanctity; it is the origin of her greatness. What dignity can be too great to attribute to her who is as closely bound up, as intimately one, with the Eternal Word, as a mother is with a son? What outfit of sanctity, what fullness and redundance of grace, what exuberance of merits must have been hers, when once we admit the supposition, which the Fathers justify, that her Maker really did regard those merits, and take them into account, when He condescended 'not to abhor the Virgin's womb'? Is it surprising then that on the one hand she should be immaculate in her Conception?

Belief of Catholics that she is Theotokos   *Diff* II p. 262–3 (Letter to the Duke of Norfolk). 1874

---

1   Council of Ephesus 431

As grace was infused into Adam from the first moment of his creation, so that he never had experience of his natural poverty, till sin reduced him to it; so was grace given from the first in still ampler measure to Mary, and she never incurred, in fact, Adam's deprivation. She began where others end, whether in knowledge or in love. She was from the first clothed in sanctity, destined for perseverance, luminous and glorious in God's sight, and incessantly employed in meritorious acts, which continued till her last breath. Hers was emphatically 'the path of the just, which, as the shining light, goeth forward and increaseth even to the perfect day';[1] and sinlessness in thought, word, and deed, in small things as well as great, in venial matters as well as grievous, is surely but the natural and obvious sequel of such a beginning. If Adam might have kept himself from sin in his first state, much more shall we expect immaculate perfection in Mary.

The Glories of Mary   Mix p. 354 (Discourse 17). 1849

1   Prov 4, 18

And, O my brethren, O kind and affectionate hearts, O loving friends, should you know any one whose lot it has been, by writing or by word of mouth, in some degree to help you thus to act; if he has ever told you what you knew about yourselves, or what you did not know; has read to you your wants or feelings, and comforted you by the very reading; has made you feel that there was a higher life than this daily one, and a brighter world than that you see; or encouraged you, or sobered you, or opened a way to the inquiring, or soothed the perplexed; if what he has said or done has ever made you take interest in him, and feel well inclined towards him; remember such a one in time to come, though you hear him not, and pray for him, that in all things he may know God's will, and at all times he may be ready to fulfil it.

The Parting of Friends.   SD p. 409.   25 September, 1843

These were the final words which Newman preached from the pulpit at Littlemore.

Abbreviations

A.S.II	John Henry Newman Sermons 1824–1843, Volume II (Clarendon Press, Oxford, 1993).
B.C.P.	Book of Common Prayer.
Call	Callista.
Campaign	My Campaign in Ireland, Part I (Privately printed 1896).
CS	Catholic Sermons of Cardinal Newman, (ed.) Stephen Dessain (Burns & Oates, London, 1957).
DA	Discussion and Arguments on Various Subjects.
Dev	Essay on the Development of Christian Doctrine.
Diff II	Certain difficulties felt by Anglicans in Catholic teaching considered in twelve lectures addressed in 1850 to the Party of the Religious Movement of 1833.
Ess II	Essays Critical and Historical
GA	Grammar of Assent.
HS III	Historical Sketches, volume 3.
Idea	The Idea of a University defined and illustrated in nine discourses delivered to the Catholics of Dublin and in occasional lectures and essays addressed to members of the Catholic Univerisity.
Jfc	Lectures on the Doctrine of Justification
LD	Letters and Diaries of John Henry Newman (ed.) Stephen Dessain *et al.*, vols I–VI (Oxford 1978–84), XI–XXII (London 1961–72), XXIII–XXXI (Oxford 1973–1977).
MD	Meditations and Devotions.
Mix	Discourses addressed to Mixed Congregations.
OS	Sermons preached on Various Occasions.
PPS I–VIII	Parochial and Plain Sermons, volumes 1–8.
Sayings	Sayings of Cardinal Newman (Burns & Oates, London, 1890).
SD	Sermons bearing on Subjects of the Day.
SN	Sermon Notes of John Henry Cardinal Newman (Longmans, London, 1913).
US	Sermons preached before the University of Oxford.
VM I	The Via Media of the Anglican Church, volume 1.
VV	Verses on Various Occasions

Books of Scripture Quoted

Gen	Genesis
Exod	Exodus
Lev	Leviticus
Num	Numbers
Deut	Deuteronomy
Josh	Joshua
Judg	Judges
1Sam	1 Samuel
2Sam	2 Samuel
1Kgs	1 Kings
2Kgs	2 Kings
1Chr	1 Chronicles
2Chr	2 Chronicles
Neh	Nehemiah
Job	Job
Ps	Psalms
Prov	Proverbs
Eccles	Ecclesiastes
Sir	Sirach/Ecclesiasticus
S of S	Songs of Songs/ Canticle of Canticles
Isa	Isaiah
Jer	Jeremiah
Lam	Lamentations
Bar	Baruch
Ezek	Ezekiel
Dan	Daniel
Hos	Hosea
Amos	Amos
Jonah	Jonah
Mic	Micah
Nahum	Nahum
Hab	Habbakuk
Zeph	Zephaniah
Hag	Haggai
Zech	Zechariah
Mal	Malachi
1Macc	1 Maccabees
2Macc	2 Maccabees

Matt	Matthew
Mark	Mark
Luke	Luke
John	John
Acts	Acts
Rom	Romans
1Cor	1 Corinthians
2Cor	2 Corinthians
Gal	Galatians
Eph	Ephesians
Phil	Philippians
Col	Colossians
1Thess	1 Thessalonians
2Thess	2 Thessalonians
1Tim	1 Timothy
2Tim	2 Timothy
Titus	Titus
Philem	Philemon
Heb	Hebrews
Jas	James
1Pet	1 Peter
2Pet	2 Peter
1John	1 John
2John	2 John
3John	3 John
Jude	Jude
Rev	Revelation/Apocalypse

Schematic Index

Sundays of the Year	A	B	C
Ascension	II 207–208	II 210 VI 230.231	VI 224–225 *Jfc* 145
7th Easter	IV 156	VI 226–227	SD 330–331 *Ess* II 374
Pentecost	II 302.303–304	II 226–227	IV 168–169
Trinity	VI 357–358	VI 343	US 34–35
Corpus Christi	I 274 OS 86–87	SD 26.37–38 VV 360	VI 146–148
Sacred Heart	VII 104–105	VI 76.77–78 89	SN 258–259 MD 571
2nd of the Year	VII 228	II 1–2	VII 76–77 SD 31–32
3rd of the Year	VIII 20–21	GA 467–468 OS 55	SD 61 OS 126–127
4th of the Year	VI 323–324	SD 35; CS 87	SD 379–380
5th of the Year	I 152–153	III 142–143	V 8–9
6th of the Year	IV 11–12	SD 175.178–179	V 293–295
7th of the Year	SN 244–246 VII 111	CS 36–37 VIII 208–209	III 184–186
8th of the Year	V 62–63	VI 10–11	V 224–225
9th of the Year	V 185 *Mix* 232–233	SD 207–208 A.S.II 427	SD 305
10th of the Year	V 159.161	OS 140.141	SN 131–133 SD 164–165
11th of the Year	I 288–289	SD 303–304	VIII 209
12th of the Year	SD 260–261	CS 19–20.21. 28–29	OS 159–160
13th of the Year	IV 153–154	US 244–246 II 146–147	VII 90–91
14th of the Year	VII 114–115	VIII 194–196	*Mix* 45 II 239
15th of the Year	V 185 CS 43.48.52	II 301–302	IV 250–251
16th of the Year	III 127; SD 261–262	VIII 230–231	III 326–327
17th of the Year	SD 241.243–244 OS 57	VII 160–161	I 250–251 GA 114
18th of the Year	SD 317	VI 110–111	II 346–347.355
19th of the Year	US 251–252	VI 143–144	IV 321–322.323
20th of the Year	OS 62–63	II 146–147	V 296–297
21st of the Year	VII 230–231	VI 148–149 *Dev* 88–89	V 268–269
22nd of the Year	VI 88–89; OS 55	VI 301–302	VI 319–320.321
23rd of the Year	VI 197–198	SN 188;VIII 86–87	VII 100–101
24th of the Year	V 342–343	US 253	VI 21
25th of the Year	SD 11; CS 32	II 64.65 *Idea* 205	CS 107.108–109
26th of the Year	I 165–166	VI 203–205	*Mix* 113–114

Sundays of the Year	A	B	C
27th of the Year	VII 139–140	II 296–297	IV 78
28th of the Year	III 332–333	IV 12; VIII 21	V 83–84
29th of the Year	*Diff* II 200–201 II 390–391	VI 320–321	VII 205–206
30th of the Year	IV 312	II 151–152 SD 64	VIII 6–7
31st of the Year	I 134–135 OS 25–26	SN 133 VIII 201–202	VII 168–169
32nd of the Year	IV 320. 323–324. 325	HS III 130 IV 302–303	1 272. 273–274
33rd of the Year	V 213–214. 184–185	DA 102–103	DA 93–94. 106
34th of the Year Christ the King	II 321–322	II 267	III 149.151

*henceforth *PPS* omitted before numerals

Feast Days and Holydays of Obligation

	A	B	C
The Presentation	II 110.133		
St Patrick	IV 306. *Idea* 482 HS III 265		
St Joseph	*Diff* II 30–31; SD 32		
The Annunciation	V 92–93		
S. John the Baptist	V 153		
St Peter and St Paul	*Sayings* 60–61 *Campaign* 211–212		
The Transfiguration	*Mix* 92–93	III 265–267	VII 81–82
The Assumption of Our Lady	*Mix* 372–373 *Diff* II 63; MD 93		
The Triumph of the Cross	VI 70.86		
All Saints	II 393–394		
Dedication of the Lateran Basilica	II 34		
Immaculate Conception of Our Lady	*Diff* II 262–263 *Mix* 354		